Noëlle Duck
Photographs by Christian Sarramon

PROVENCE STYLE
THE ART OF HOME DECORATION

Flammarion

CONTENTS

INTRODUCTION

Entrance to the villa Mas
Dargent in Saint-Rémy
(*page* 2). Boutis fabric (*page
4*) is a decorative element in
its own right. This pattern is
by Le Rideau de Paris.

The Provençal home is in perfect harmony with its surroundings. It is south facing, not to welcome the sun but to turn its back on the Mistral, the bitter north wind that blows in furious gusts. Under a roof of various shades of pink, the color of the clay of the Roman tiles, the tall windows are framed in roughcast or bare stonework, and are protected by heavy shutters painted in bright colors.

Provence has no set color scheme, but the walls are usually ocher, a shade echoed in the woodwork.

The polished floors display their soft brilliance, and glazed tableware sheds its reflections on a printed cotton tablecloth. In the bedrooms, closets carved with flowers and shells are reflected in the gilt-framed mirrors that hang over the mantelpiece.

Provence has always produced its own materials for building, painting, remodeling, furnishing, and decorating the home. For two thousand years, with the help of other cultures, its craftsmen have created the unique style of Provence design and decoration.

The farandole dancer, a favorite *santon* (Christmas figurine) from Marseilles, graces the mantelpiece in many Provençal homes *(page 4, in Grasse).*

A HOME IN THE SUN

A traveler will always know when he has reached Provence as soon as the first stone houses come into view, their gently sloping roofs covered in Roman tiles in muted colors. Somewhere near Montelimar, the gateway to the Land of the Mistral, the walls begin to be built of bare, golden stones piled roughly on top of each other, giving houses of the Drôme the look of sheepfolds. Farther to the south, there are the *bastides*, elegant farmhouses glimpsed between the cool greenery of the trees that huddle around them. The bright or pastel colors of the stuccoed frontages of village houses stand out amid the trees lining the streets, looking like a Neapolitan ice cream with their raspberry, peach, and green almond hues. Before reaching the Camargue, whose little houses look like upturned boats covered with thatched roofs, the visitor will notice the stone country houses with pale lavender or deep olive shutters; these dot the landscape around Aix-en-Provence, between the Alpilles and the Luberon. A land of sun, wind, and heat, southern France is also a land of stone, ocher, and terra-cotta.

The heavy shutters often consist of two thicknesses of wood *(facing page)*, with a layer of vertical planks overlaying a horizontal layer. Vauvenargues *(above)*, rising from among the trees in the Aix-en-Provence district, is a cross between a *bastide* and a château. Picasso lived here and is buried here.

THE HOUSE

An avenue of plane trees leads to the cool mansion, concealing its secrets. If the house stands by the sea, date palms, whose heavy bunches of orange fruits will never ripen, may form a stiff, evergreen colonnade on the steep hillside. Or there may be young pine trees, almost certainly planted by an outsider, because the local people dislike this tree that bursts into flame so readily, flinging out burning branches that can set light to anything within miles. In the Camargue, however, in the arid plain of La Crau where forest fires are an impossibility, a clump of umbrella pines offering shade to a solitary *mas* is revered like a sacred grove.

Provençal houses are always surrounded by trees, just as once they always had a well. Even the humblest of stone huts, in the middle of nowhere, will be marked by the green splash of a plane, mulberry, or linden tree, rising above the grapevines to provide the residents with a little shade at the hottest time of day. The sign of human habitation in Provence is always a patch of greenery: sometimes a tall cane or cypress hedge protecting fields of melons or eggplant; sometimes a massive, untidy clump of wild mimosa. Most important of all are the cypress trees, the traditional trees of welcome, planted by the entrance, usually in pairs.

The cypresses that protect gardens from the Mistral are also signs of welcome, as in
this case where they grace the house of Édith Mézard at Lumières (*facing page*). Near Sablet, a
house with several outbuildings is surrounded by vineyards (*above left*). Light plays on the front of
a house formerly owned by British designer Terence Conran (*overleaf*).

TYPES OF PROVENÇAL HOUSE

The villa set among palm trees looks nothing like the *bastide* shaded by plane trees, or the *mazet* (little farmhouse) overlooking the valley, protected by cork oaks and with its back to the Mistral. Nor does the village house resemble the *bâtisse*, an ancient, tumbledown building whose original purpose has been forgotten.

THE BASTIDE is an imposing country house or farmhouse. From the fifteenth century onward its name has always referred to a substantial property in the country. Such properties were inhabited by nobles, by the wealthiest families of Aix-en-Provence, by landowners and winery proprietors. The landscape around Aix, and the vineyards of the Var district contain many such impressive residences, which bear a passing resemblance to Palladian villas, with their square shape, four-sided roofs, stone dados, and simple, elegant forms.

Some bastides are "follies," miniature châteaux set in gardens in which fountains play. These were clearly built as country retreats. Others are just two-story dwellings, but all have tall windows with small windowpanes that are rigorously symmetrical, and identical in shape on the first and second floors. The windows are designed to let in plenty of air in the summer. A *bastide* may have a third story, used as an

The main wing *(left)* of the 16th-century Domaine de Rhode, Avignon, a former hunting lodge. The 18th-century windows with their bubble-glass panes have been preserved.

15

attic or as servants' sleeping quarters. The space is lit by a row of small square or circular windows framed by stone cladding or, more rarely, by a brick surround.

The front door is often imposing, and is positioned symmetrically in the center of the façade. Three steps may lead up to it. The doorway is reinforced with stone slabs, topped by two cornerstones to accentuate the keystone. These door-frames can still be found through dealers in architectural features, some removed from buildings that are little more than stone huts.

The *bastides* owned by middle-class families tend to be plainer and less pretentious than those owned by nobility, and remain largely unchanged. The beautifully balanced proportion of the façade does not overpower the outbuildings, which have been added to compensate for the lack of cellars.

The term *bastide* has been wrongly applied to smaller, dilapidated stone buildings, which are properly known as *bastidons*. These single-story dwellings are located near villages, often by the roadside. Some have been

Ornamental drinking-fountains were traditionally sited close to the house, as here *(above)* at the Château de Beaupré, a vineyard near Aix-en-Provence. This was to enable them to be used for watering the horses. The stucco on this *mas* at Bonnieux *(facing page)* is pale ocher, a color that harmonizes well with the pastel shades of the shutters.

converted into antiques stores, but because of their close proximity and easy access to the villages, they also make delightful guesthouses.

TOWNHOUSES The townhouses of the well-to-do were intended to show the wealth and good taste of the owner, and they do not always look typically Provençal. They were often owned by senior judges, powerful civil servants, and even noblemen attending the French court at Versailles. The architecture of these seventeenth- and eighteenth-century houses was based on Parisian styles, but adapted to the Provençal setting and climate. They were decorated by local and regional artists, craftsmen and sculptors (Pierre Puget and his school), ironsmiths, and cabinet-makers, whose originality gave them a reputation that stretched as far as Paris.

The door is flanked by columns, and male and female figures seem to be supporting the central balcony. This balcony is larger than the rest, and is reminiscent of the loggias of Venetian palazzos, designed to enable people to watch the world go by, and to be used as an extension to the brilliantly lit reception room behind. The tall french windows lead onto small, narrow balconies, whose wrought-iron balustrades look light and fragile so as not to spoil the style of the façade. The mansions in the old quarter of Aix-en-Provence, and those that line the main street, the Cours Mirabeau, are greatly admired by summer visitors, who gaze at the wrought-ironwork that was the pride of local craftsmen. The tall

The Château de Barbentane in the Alpilles (*facing page*), the Provençal equivalent of Versailles. Grotesque masks (*top*) and atlantes—supporting male figures (*above*) have embellished the fountains and grand entrances of Aix since the Renaissance. A range of 18th-century portals and balconies (*overleaf*). Ironwork is an important decorative element of *bastides* and townhouses.

french windows of the townhouses belonging to the nobility, like those of the most elegant *bastides*, are shutterless on the outside, but have solid wooden shutters inside to protect the privacy of the inhabitants.

MAS, MAZETS, AND CABANONS These are less ostentatious but nevertheless delightful dwellings. The stone façade is covered with crumbling, faded, but authentic plasterwork, through which the original stonework is visible in places, prompting the question: should all the plaster be removed, exposing the bare stonework, or should it be repaired, restored, and painted ocher? The woodwork, doors, and shutters are painted in a contrasting color, the window-frames usually being coated in white gloss paint. Houses that have been too heavily restored and have that "good-as-new" look should be shunned: it is the opposite of the lived-in look that is typically Provençal. Restoration should be discreet and modest, to blend in with the stone-and-brick constructions that are the legacy of the Roman occupation; it was Roman architects who introduced these styles.

A *mas* is a farmhouse, or some sort of farming concern. In Provence a farm does not have pastures on which cattle roam, or vast fields of grain. Instead, the *mas* owner grows herbs, spring vegetables or tomatoes, peppers, eggplant, and melons, and also tends small orchards of peach, apricot, apple, and pear trees. In the

This guesthouse *(right)* in Lauris, Vaucluse, is a former *mas* that has preserved its original plasterwork beneath a triple row of *génoises (see page 42)*. The various styles of building are harmonized through the lavender-blue paint on the shutters.

Camargue, the *mas* is the home of the owner of the *manade*, the ranch on which fighting-bulls are reared. If a *mas* is large it often has a number of outbuildings, which surround the main building in a horseshoe shape. This produces an assortment of different roof heights.

In the Camargue the living rooms are on the ground floor and the bedrooms on the floor above. In the districts of Haut-Var and Alpes de Haute-Provence the ground floor is low-ceilinged. It may be used for storage; again there are no cellars, because it is impossible to dig them out of the rocky terrain. The occupants live on the upper floor, or rather on a mezzanine, accessible via an outside staircase, the main entrance being protected by a small stoop. This type of building offers many architectural possibilities, and a pleasant life on a single floor, above ground level. The windows are plain with small panes, or in two sections when they are more modern, and are sometimes protected by solid shutters.

A *mazet* is a little *mas*; like most diminutives, it is also used as a term of endearment. This single-story farm building sometimes has storage for farm machinery. It comes with a small plot of land and may have been built for a young farming couple, or given to a tenant-farmer. In the Camargue the word describes a low, white-washed building with a thatched roof, built with its back to the Mistral. These were once occupied by watchmen.

In Gordes, Roussillon, and Ramatuelle, the doors of the village houses are framed by carved stone lintels *(facing page far left)*; near Saint-Rémy, the stonework and woodwork around the doors and windows of these farm buildings *(left)* have been painted with a milk-white lime wash.

CABANONS AND BORIES A *cabanon* is a miniature house, designed as a place where farmworkers, toiling in the fields, could rest at the hottest times of day. With its well-balanced proportions, it can be converted into a delightful vacation retreat. It is almost always built of exposed stonework with a two-sided, pitched, slightly overhanging roof with no eaves. The façade has no embellishment other than the arched door-frame, made of stone blocks, which may date from the eighteenth or nineteenth century. If there are any windows at all, they are tiny. It is a good idea to visit these places on a windy day to be sure they are sited to give maximum protection.

There are also *cabanons* that were originally built as weekend homes for urban families of modest means, mainly from Marseilles or Toulon. They were often used as an escape from the stifling heat of the city, or as beach chalets; they could be used to house a few chairs and a table, deckchairs, and a tripod to hold a soup pot in which to cook a bouillabaisse. That is the origin of the *cabanons* along the *calanques* (inlets) at Sormiou, between Marseilles and Cassis, and those on the Giens peninsula. They were always shaded by pine trees for siestas, and situated near water so that the children could play.

The *bories* are found deep in the Luberon. They are round huts of dry stonework, like the houses in the Gordes region. There is nothing typically Provençal about their architecture and materials: they are even found in the Vendée. They were mere toolsheds, and places for sheep to shelter during a storm, as can be seen by the very low opening. They were probably never used for living in. They are a quaint vestige of how Provençal country folk lived, but could not possibly be converted into a home.

The *cabanons (top* and *facing page)*, were used for storing tools and small items of farm equipment, and provided a cool resting place in the heat of the day. The *bories (above)* were never lived in, as can be seen from the very low openings. They were used for storage or as sheepfolds during storms.

OLD VILLAGE OR CITY HOUSES The largest of the old village or city houses were often occupied by an order of nuns, by prominent people, or by leading families. Sometimes they were the home of wealthy craftsmen or merchants, who lived over the store. They are stone built, but they are plastered so that only the cornerstones are exposed. They are often tall, to capture as much as possible of the dim light of the narrow streets. Inland the shutters are solid, but toward the sea they are louvered, and in the Nice region they take the form of jalousies—shutters that have adjustable louvers to let in light and air while keeping out rain or sun. In Nice and along the Ligurian Coast they may also take the form of partisols. These are louvered shutters made in two parts, so that the upper part can be opened to allow cool air to circulate while the bottom part remains closed.

The old parts of town have eye-catching entrances. They are made of expensive hardwood, and are framed by a stone lintel. The single door is decorated with moldings and is always painted. Unfortunately the elaborate polished brass or painted iron knockers that once graced them have largely disappeared, having been stolen at night or sold to passing dealers.

The front door opens onto a staircase that leads straight to the upper floors, without connecting to the ground floor. There is often a garden, which is invisible from the street, as well as a tiny terrace, recessed beneath the eaves of the roof.

The fishermen's houses at Martigues or on the canal de Beaucaire at Tarascon have largely become artists' colonies. They were built at the waterside, facing the quay, huddled together in a row. Although painted in

contrasting colors, their two-story façades are identical, and they make an attractive terrace of houses. The rooms occupied by day are on the ground floor, so that when the windows are open the inhabitants can chat to passers-by. Ideally, fishing boats belonging to the owners could be moored right in front of the house, as they are in Port-Grimaud.

Windows overlooking the street: in Saint-Tropez *(left)*, where the tall, narrow houses, bombed in World War II, have been restored to their former glory; or in the Musée Souleiado at Tarascon *(above)*; or *(overleaf)* at Hyères, Nice, Aix, and Grasse, where the iron bars of the oculus (round or bull's eye window) compensate for the absence of shutters.

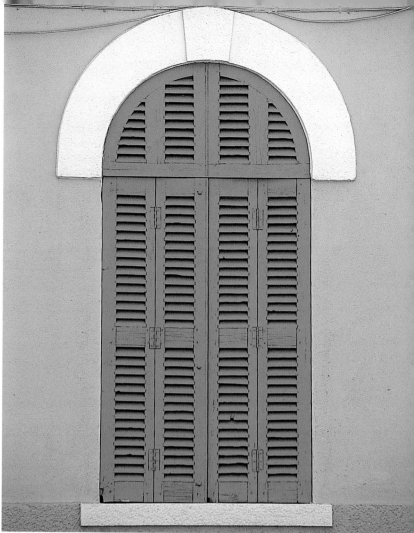

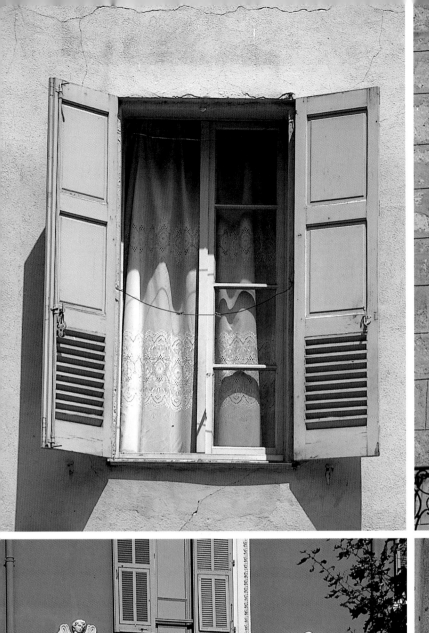

To restore the original style and character to a Provençal house, it is a good idea to frequent antique and junk stores, and yards dealing in recycled architectural materials—including roof tiles. Mixing pigments in large quantities to get just the right shade for the plaster is a highly skilled job, as is removing dilapidated plaster, without damaging the stones underneath, to create an exposed stone frontage. However, it is possible to take courses where you can learn all aspects of restoring and remodeling a house; these are run by experts in traditional techniques who can guide the amateur and prevent any serious errors.

STONE On inside and outside walls, it is stone that keeps the house upright and gives it its imposing façade—as pale as the girls of Arles, who are careful never to expose themselves to the sun. There are few plains in Provence; the terrain is usually rugged and hilly. This means that the house needs protecting from the crumbling of the slopes above, which are liable to collapse in cascades of boulders that roll down the hills; these are easily torn from the friable, barren earth, especially after forest fires. The house is shielded by building up protective embankments on which only olive and fig trees grow. These embankments are called *banquettes* in Drôme and *restanques* farther south. They are shored up with dry-stone walls, the stones of which are recovered from cultivated fields or from the *restanques* themselves. The embankments are so vital that people are being taught to restore them in the traditional way.

A pigeon-loft may be part of the farmhouse building as here at Varages in Var *(right)*, or separate like those *(above left)* where the flight holes or stonework are decorated with ceramic tiles.

Stone is used for all types of houses because the local limestone, which stretches from the sea to the foothills of the Alps, is easily available raw material. The stone was quarried and the quarries were free, meaning that—provided they extracted it themselves—anyone who needed stone could simply take it. When peasants cleared the stones that littered their fields, they would store them for future construction use.

The quarry on the route des Crêtes at Bormes-les-Mimosas, a lovely hilltop village in Var Maritime, will soon be opening again. It used to provide schist, a blood-red sandstone sprinkled with gold that used to be cut in the form of ingots. On the Estérel coast at Bandol, it was used for building houses that blended seamlessly into the landscape. It is a perfect match, and is also used for garden walls. The porch and woodwork is painted in white gloss or the natural is stained to a darker hue; this completes the look of these houses whose color is that of the very heart of the hills.

Bormes stone was the ideal material for some of the listed buildings beside the sea, where houses were only allowed to have one floor: the color made them almost invisible. Along the banks of the Durance, and in the foothills of the Alpilles where the River Rhône once ran, there is a wonderful deposit of smooth pebbles that are perfect for the façades and walls of drystone enclosures, especially when they are tinted red by silica deposits, as in the Châteauneuf-du-Pape district.

The houses and *bories* (shepherd's huts) in the hilltop village of Gordes in the Vaucluse (*left* and *right*), are built entirely from the local limestone. No mortar is used, because the area lacked the quarries in which it could be made. This is known as drystone construction.

Nowadays, anyone wanting to build a house in the Provençal style may be put off by the cost of stone slabs, but modern materials can always be used as long as they are covered in smooth plaster, uniformly colored with one of the acceptable shades of ocher. This amount of conservation is possible thanks to the craftsmen, painters, and stonemasons who have studied the traditional techniques. As elsewhere in France, new building work must match the traditional styles. In Provence, this means curved Roman roof tiles, old or new, hand- or machine-made, and walls painted in traditional hues. (Who was the bureaucrat who imposed pinkish-beige in the 1970s? It must have been the same person who stopped the building of "California-style" seaside villas in that mixture of the styles of Mallet-Stevens (the architect of the Villa Noailles at Hyères), of Le Corbusier, and of the villas on the West Coast of the United States, which let in the light and let the air circulate freely.)

It is true that in the 1970s ocher had fallen out of favor. This is when the Provençal style (fabrics, wallpaper, ceramics, bead curtains, and so on), especially among the middle classes, had the connotation of tackiness: "modern" and "Parisian" were all the rage. In the

same way people seemed to become ashamed to own a *petit pointu*, a little wooden boat, which was soon replaced by a craft made of plastic.

The same movement was keen to cover old houses with a fresh coat of plaster. Some of these buildings were very old, with lovely proportions, high ceilings, and stone frontages covered with smooth plasterwork that dated from the late nineteenth century. They were modernized by being coated with pinkish-beige plaster, thrown on with a trowel, or deliberately roughened to give a "rustic" look. Woodwork on doors, windows, and old shutters was painted a glossy white, and sometimes replaced by anodized aluminum! The historic districts of the cities of Provence lost all their style, charm, and authenticity. Places such as Cotignac, standing against its hill; Saint-Paul-de-Vence with its little squares with their fountains; the bright red façades of old Nice; the Cours Mirabeau in Aix-en-Provence; the quays of Les Martigues; the "rusty houses" of which Charles Trénet sang—all these were seen as museum pieces.

Fortunately, they have served as examples. In Port-Grimaud, the architect François Spoerry, inspired by the houses of Burano, the lace-makers' island in the Venice lagoon, restored the colors. The belltower at Saint-Tropez, whose soft ocher hues are identical to the original shades, has become the archetype for the color scheme of the South of France. It can be hoped that the Provençal house, whose unique style has been shaped by history and the contingencies of the climate, has finally been rescued from pastiche and disfiguration.

The advantages and charm of tinted ocher plaster, as seen in Roussillon *(facing page* and *left)*. The plaster never looks conspicuously new and is not bleached by the sun.

Roofs These always slope gently. Because there is little rainfall in Provence, the rain does not need to drain off rapidly. Moreover, the roof needs to present the least possible wind resistance. The roof tiles need to be laid in the opposite direction to that of the prevailing wind. The roofs of mansions, *bastides*, and aristocratic townhouses are almost always four-sided. This architecture is the privilege of the well-to-do: the framework is complicated and so more expensive than for two-sided roofs.

Mas, *bastidons*, and the farmhouses of some of the more prosperous vineyards have two-sided roofs that overlap the frontages. Under the gables, there is a circular window to illuminate the attic, and often a horizontal pantile or even a little molded cornice to add interest to the plain sidewalls.

Detached houses in the countryside all conform to strict rules. The front entrance must be south facing, letting in plenty of sunshine and light, which is filtered by the trees in summer. Above all, it must be sheltered from the wind. The north-facing frontage has much smaller openings and the gables are blind because the Mistral and Tramontane blow from the north and west respectively, and the rain comes from the east.

Village houses usually have one or two rooms per floor and are three or four stories high. They are narrow, and generally terraced or in rows. The roof is a pitched lean-to, without a *génoise (see page 42)*, but with a deep overhang to protect the frontage, or a little terrace used for drying laundry or for growing fruits and vegetables.

Roman or channel tiles, hand-molded in local clay, come in a variety of colors *(left* and *right)*. Covered in moss and lichen, pitted, and patinated, they have the charm of old pottery.

The houses are of different heights and, viewed from above, the roofs present an ancient patchwork, the lines broken by the various angles and directions of roof pitch, sometimes spiraling around a church or château. There is nothing to spoil the monochrome of drystone walls and terra-cotta, so typical of the part of Drôme that is in Provence, and of the départements of Alpes de Haute-Provence and the numerous hilltop villages such as La Cadière, Lacoste, Le Castellet, or Forcalquieret.

The Roman tile is a semi-cylinder of terra-cotta, whose color depends upon the type of local clay used to make it. The tiles are laid in overlapping rows to ensure that they remain waterproof, alternating with upturned or flat tiles, the latter being fixed to the roof-beams and called the "run-off" tiles. Roman-tiled roofs need to be consolidated and ventilated so that the clay does not snap at extremes of temperature, so they ought to be insulated from the roofbeams. The traditional technique for achieving this is called "Arlesian roofing," and involves filling the spaces beneath the covering tiles with Provence cane (which is neither bamboo nor reed, but the stalks of cereals). This is tied in thin bunches and attached at certain points by spots of lime mortar. The air can circulate lengthwise between the canes which, if well aerated, will not rot.

This roofing technique, which builders have stopped using, has been revived by the Monuments Historiques organization for the restoration of ancient buildings, especially in Arles and Marseilles. As an excellent contemporary solution using ancient know-how—which was perfectly adapted for use on channel tiles—it deserves to be reinstated for use in private homes, since the raw material is abundant and inexpensive. The best

Provence cane grows in cane-fields only about 12 miles (20 km) from the sea, benefiting from the action of wind and sun to grow sturdy and strong.

The roofs of Provence, like these at Ménerbes in the heart of the Luberon (*facing page*), or in a street in Villecroze in the Haut Var (*above*), do not overhang greatly, a sign that there is little rain here. The large building with the white shutters was once lived in by the painter Nicolas de Staël.

GÉNOISES *Génoises* are single, double, triple, or even quadruple rows of upturned Roman tiles that are fixed to walls below the roofline and help to deflect rain from the walls. Anyone lucky enough to find this elegant feature beneath the eaves of the roof should never install a gutter between them and the roof tiles, as their very function is to avoid the use of guttering. Gables do not have *génoises* beneath them, though the roof will often overhang by several rows of tiles at the gable ends.

There are two types of *génoise*, hollow or filled, depending on whether the tiles rest on mortar or on *malons*, known as *maloun* in Provençal. Malons are squares of enameled tile. Rectangular terra-cotta tiles are interspersed lengthwise between the rows of *génoises*, or even Roman tiles, a souvenir of the 1950s fashion that found them everywhere on balconies, terraces, and garden walls.

Despite the name, which means Genoese, *génoises* are rare on houses in Nice, a city that was once under Italian rule. Here the *genoises* are replaced by deep overhangs of tiles attached to semi-circular rafters, beneath which the walls are decorated with italianate frescoes. Townhouses in Aix-en-Provence and Arles, *bastides*, certain old *mas*, or the large square nineteenth-century village houses built by prosperous local dignitaries are often embellished with plaster or stone cornices.

Génoises are laid at the top of walls under the roof
to prevent water running onto the façade.
They may be between one and three rows in depth
and built on channel tiles *(top right, facing page)*;
or they may be made of masonry *(left* and *facing page)*.

DOORS Openings naturally depend on the location of the house and the style of its façade. But they have one thing in common: they are always larger when south facing, because in this direction they are facing away from the Mistral wind and the dust. They can also welcome in the penetrating light from the winter sun, which is very low on the horizon at that time of year.

The *bastides* typically have tall french windows with small panes. The *mas* and other types of country house have plain casement windows with two panes; this same design can be used to make french windows in traditionally built villas. Wherever necessary, and so that the windows can be kept open, especially during the summer heat, there is a second frame—between the window and the shutters—where flyscreens can be fitted. A little brass window-catch operates the rod by which the flyscreen is attached to the main frame.

Everywhere, except in the homes of dignitaries and noblemen, the front door was protected by beaded curtains that served a multiplicity of purposes. They let air enter while leaving the flies outside, made it possible to leave the front door open while maintaining a sense of privacy, brought some shade to a south-facing corridor, and made it possible to see anyone coming to the door without being seen. The bead curtain was rather inconvenient, though, and today is rarely hung in well-used doorways. It can still be used as a lovely decorative object, or to cover a door that is never opened. To preserve it in spirit, a curtain of light material—cheesecloth or muslin, for example—can be used to cover the doorway. It will move at the slightest breath of air, but will preserve the privacy of the interior and will be a delightful and practical feature.

Aix-en-Provence is a living museum of architecture, in which all the various styles are represented. The magnificent studded door of the Villa Gallici *(facing page)* and the central balcony of the Hôtel Panisse, with its lovely 18th-century curving wrought-ironwork *(above)*. The arched lintel of the french window, with its central *mascaron* (grotesque mask) echoes the design of the grand entrance immediately below. A variety of handsome front doors and entrances adorn village houses *(overleaf)*.

45

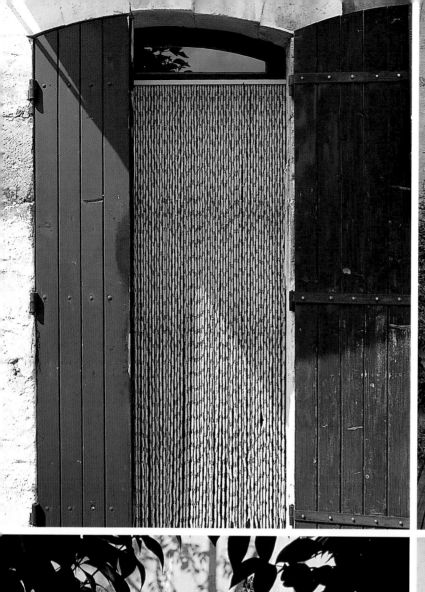

INTERIORS

Outdoors, beyond the shady garden, the burning sun, and the gusting Mistral, the utter dryness of summer prevails. Only the half-closed shutters and the thin muslin curtain screening the open front door help to block out the heat. Once over the threshold, the cool, pale ocher walls, terra-cotta tiled floors, and stone stairs combine to help one gradually cool down from the stifling heat.

In winter, flames from the burning logs are reflected in the china and pewter; they make the polished marble glow, and trace grotesque shapes on the beamed ceiling. The effect of the sun-yellow or burnt-sienna walls is cooling in summer, warming in winter. The kitchen is tiled with bright ceramic squares from Salernes. Turning from an inspection of the distant hills through the tiny kitchen window—the back door remains resolutely shut—one re-enters the world of subtly harmonious shades and textures, so comple-mentary that they create an atmosphere more than a style. The materials are simple yet noble: wood, stone, clay, and wrought iron, forever linked with Provence, from its urban mansions to its solitary farmhouses.

Bastides and mansions have white stone stairs; everywhere else the risers and steps are tiled with *tomettes* (terra-cotta tiles), and the steps and noses are of wood. The handrail and balustrade may be of stone *(facing page)*, of cast iron and wood *(above)*, or of wrought iron.

49

LIVING ROOMS

Two contrasting interiors: the paneling on the interior shutters of the Château d'Ansouis *(above),* has been freshly painted; while the kitchen of a family home *(facing page),* has stripped pine woodwork and simple furnishings, with a modern kitchen stove installed in the fireplace.

The single entrance of the south-facing Provençal house leads directly either into the main living room or, if it has more than one story, into a tiny hallway from which the staircase leads. This room may open into the reception room, kitchen, or even a study. It is often neutral, or at least muted in relation to the decoration that can be glimpsed through the doorways. It may be very elegant, as at the Château de Barbentane, where it sets the opulent tone for the whole interior.

After that, the rooms are arranged in whatever order is most natural. The kitchen, scullery, and its cafoucho (a pantry or deep storage space) stands on one side—it sometimes has a small door leading to the outside—and bedrooms on the other. In his book, *Les Maisons provençales,* Jean-Luc Massot, an architect from Aix-en-Provence who specializes in the restoration of the local houses, writes: "There is no leeway, no superfluous space, everything seems to merge into a single unit, both on the horizontal plane—the plan—and on the vertical plane—the elevations.... Each of the spaces works as part of the whole. One could not remove any of them without damaging the whole: this is the proof of completeness and maturity."

Although, since the eighteenth century, the *bastides* have had a separate dining room, the *mas* and village houses have a large drawing room and a room that serves as a combination kitchen–dining room. This arrangement is a traditional one, but it is also very convenient and has been retained by many new owners.

On the upper floor, the best bedrooms are always those that are south facing.

Elaborate plasterwork and *rocaille* (rock- and shellwork) in
the Château de Barbentane: the shell-and-flower theme
is repeated on the gilded wood-framed mirror,
the multicolored marble mantelpiece and its overmantel,
and on the armchairs and wing-chairs.

DECORATIVE ELEMENTS

These traditional plaster and wood ceilings, found in homes that were built for and by the peasant classes *(above* and *facing page)*, are known as coffered ceilings.

CEILINGS Ceilings are finished with cornices and friezes; they often have exposed beams and are sometimes brightly colored. However, they may be white, to give a more classic, natural light to a room, allowing the furnishings and fabrics to contribute brilliance. In the entrance to a house with several stories, whether a townhouse or a *bastide*, all attention is on the staircase, which winds around its light, ethereal wrought-iron handrail and balustrading. In such a house, the ceilings and walls of the entrance hall—which is often a room of modest proportions since it is wasted space— are painted in the same pale ocher, or whitewashed for purity, in order to highlight the flooring of terra-cotta or marble, and the dark red tiles on the steps of the stairs.

In the living rooms the ceilings are finished with cornices or, if the walls were designed to be papered, with curved edging. The cornices may be of plain plaster or wooden moldings, and form the junction between the walls and the ceilings. If painted in strong colors, as the interior designer Frédéric Mechiche chose to do in his house at Vieux Hyères, they add focus to a room and make the ceilings look higher. Below these moldings there are sometimes painted landscapes or frescoes, the equivalent of the painted canvases and scenic wallpaper that decorate the *hôtels particuliers* (town mansions). In the nineteenth century, wealthy farmers would often ask a local artist or journeymen painter to decorate their homes in this way.

The salon or parlor is the room for special occasions and family gatherings. In some houses, the ceilings are

beautifully decorated in plasterwork; in others, where the beams are close together, they are painted with patterns. Local artists adapted the ornate style of Versailles, which was too elaborate for Provence, by using darker colors and italianate garlands and swags. It is not unusual to find ceilings whose painted beams are in good condition: small windows have protected them from light, and there is scarcely any humidity in this climate. Such ceilings should be preserved, or professionally renovated. If they are damaged and peeling and the colors have been darkened by smoke from the fire, today's simpler tastes and less lavish budgets mean that the tendency is toward simplicity. A wonderful effect can be achieved by harmonizing the colors of the ceiling with those of the walls: white for the plasterwork, olive green or burnt sienna for the beams, all in matte paint. In a room in which the stonework of a wall has been exposed, the ceiling can be a source of color and the main decorative element. Ceilings with several rows of beams, known as plastered beams, have plaster molding that link them crosswise; these are called gypseries. Coffered ceilings have two rows of beams at right angles to each other, the rectangular spaces in between being called coffers.

The bedrooms, which are really just used for taking a siesta or for sleeping in at night, are much less elaborately decorated than the reception rooms. The ceiling is often painted, plastered, or whitewashed in white, to induce a peaceful sleep.

In the lean-tos, sheds, and outbuildings, as well as those covered terraces—converted from a barn whose walls have fallen down—or in the *bugade* (laundry), whose stone sink has often been preserved, the ceilings are often lined with a layer of whole canes, placed between the rafters and the roofbeams. These hollow canes make for excellent insulation material.

Sheepfolds, which are often converted into nurseries, children's rooms, or guest rooms, have ceilings that are low and arched. The stonework can either be completely exposed, although this involves a lot of work, or the plasterwork restored, as on the house façades, allowing the stonework to show through on corners and creating an elegant and authentic result.

The fireplace *(facing page)* was a focus of everyday life in the Provençal home. It could be used for grilling and roasting, and often, as here, had an adjacent hob. The armchairs are by Vincent Mit l'Âne. Renaissance cariatyds *(above)* support the overmantel at Château de Lourmarin, in Vaucluse.

FIREPLACES A Provençal house needed a large fireplace in the living room, dining room, or kitchen; besides providing warmth and an attractive focal point, it was important for cooking. The fireplace was used for spit-roasting, the spit being attached to large andirons and turned mechanically. It could also be used for grilling cutlets, kabobs, and fish. The grate, which was high enough not to give the grill-chef backache, still comes into its own in the fall and in winter, of course, when game is in season and there are plenty of vine prunings to be used as kindling. Small feathered game should be spit roast, then served on slices of fresh country bread rubbed with garlic.

Kitchen ranges, built into the stonework, have almost completely disappeared; they take up too much space and are no longer useful in a way they were originally. There were two types of range, one with a grate in the center in which the fire was built. A iron tripod was placed over the fire and a cauldron set to cook on it. Embers were removed with tongs to heat the hob. The hob itself was set into an adjacent alcove, and tiled with earthenware tiles. It held a stewpot in which a beef stew (*daube*) or civet of hare could slowly simmer until it was rich and smooth, while in the oven beneath a *tian* of vegetables would be baked. These huge fireplaces were fitted with various alcoves and storage areas for logs, kitchen utensils, flameproof earthenware, and tableware,

This fireplace *(left)* has a matching overmantel in white carved stone, decorated with stone moldings, and is the main feature of this country parlor in Bonnieux. The bread oven *(facing page)* in the kitchen of the Château d'Ansouis, with its semi-circular opening.

58

and the oil flask that was always kept handy. Shallow stone or marble circular sinks known as *piles* were always placed near the kitchen fireplace for convenience.

MARBLE, WOOD, AND STONE The châteaux and mansions had fireplaces of marble in various colors, including Turquin blue marble, blue-gray Carrara marble, and a reddish-brown marble streaked with a yellow cement and known as *brèche du Tholonet* or *brèche d'Alep*, which was extracted from the Saint-Antonin or Sainte-Victoire quarries. There were also pink marble from Brignoles, red marble from Vitrolles; gray Cévenol, and marbeled stone from Tavel; *brocatelle* from the Jura and marble from Languedoc. The inventory of the firm of Mazzetty, in Avignon, shows that it was one of the local specialists in this type of marble work, which was used exclusively for mantelpieces and the tops of furniture. The Hôtel de La Mirande in Avignon is a mansion that became a hotel in the 1990s. When restored to its eighteenth-century splendor, it was found to contain a fireplace made principally of blue Turquin marble, with inlaid patterns in red Spanish marble and yellow marble. The hearth is lined with small glazed earthenware tiles from Avignon.

Bedroom chimneys were generally of plain white or even artificial marble. After the major structural work on a house had been completed, and the plasterers had finished their work, artists of all kinds would arrive: specialists in *trompe-l'œil* to create wood and marble effects, artists who painted on canvas, those who produced patina on furniture, and other craftsmen adding stucco and marble, mirrors and gilding. Some of the small, marble, geometric-shape fireplaces installed in the nineteenth-century have no grace or style, and they are best replaced by a wooden fireplace, preferably of well-polished walnut whose patina is evidence of its age.

The best fireplaces are as beautifully carved as wooden furniture. The fronts are curved and sinuous, decorated with a raised, stylized Arles cockleshell, as well as with leaves, fruits, and flowers. From the mid-eighteenth century, fireplaces were flat-fronted and fluted. In both cases, they echoed the designs of the furniture. Such fireplaces are collectors' items, highly sought after from specialist dealers. Dealers also sell firedogs, andirons, and hearth backplates in decorative cast iron, sometimes bearing a coat of arms.

It is still possible to find stone fireplaces, but they are rarer than marble ones. In the *bastides* or homes of wealthy farmers they were often very large. There are examples at the Mas Calendal at Cassis, and in the home of the poet Frédéric Mistral at Maillane, now a museum. The mantel was tall, rounded or triangular, and plastered. Eighteenth-century examples are more heavily worked in dressed stone, with bowed uprights. Sometimes there is a decorative motif in the center of the mantelshelf, often a stylized cockleshell; the overmantel may be decorated with flowers or a Beaucaire mirror in a gilt wood frame.

Many craftsmen sell Provençal-style fireplaces in carved wood or stone (see detail *above* by Alain Gauthey of Salernes).
The plaster fireplace (*facing page*) is very deep, so as to ensure the smoke is channeled up the flue; the overmantel is of antique and gilded wood and depicts a maritime scene.

STAIRCASES The staircases of Provence, whether of white stonework wound around an elegant balustrade of eighteenth-century wrought iron, or of straight rows of ceramic tiles edged with a nose of polished oak, contribute much to the charm of the interior.

In the *bastides* around Aix-en-Provence and the homes of the wealthy, the staircase was wide, often with half-landings, and edged with high balustrading, with a wrought-iron frieze replacing banisters. The string, to which the balustrading is fixed, was often cut from a single piece of oak; in less well-to-do houses, it was of cement. The balustrading consisted of square sections of wrought iron, plain or worked, or of elegant patterns that echoed those of the balconies. Wrought-ironwork has always been a craft appreciated in Provence; the skills involved have been transmitted across generations of families. Some practitioners have become widely known, such as Alexis Benoît of Avignon, who produced the balustrading for the staircases and balconies of the Hôtel Forbin de Sainte-Croix, currently the prefecture.

The beauty of a staircase is often enhanced by the light radiating from a skylight, a lamp, or even a chandelier on a long chain. The steps of the staircase, if not of white stone or marble, and especially in the Nice district, are made of ceramic tiles, whether in country or town houses. The riser is of cement, often coated in dark brown plaster. Although the hardest oak wood was used for the noses of the steps, it has still usually worn away, becoming hollowed out in front of the tiles.

The patina of the polished oak and uniform brilliance of the tiles was the pride and joy of the housewives of Provence. A traditional staircase in good condition is a

real find: applying a little polish to the wrought iron, some red wax on the tiles, and plenty of beeswax on the oak should help it regain its brilliant shine.

The unusual double spiral staircase at the Château de Lourmarin *(facing page, bottom left)*, and three other contemporary staircases. The wrought-iron balustrading of the mansions of Aix-en-Provence are models of lightness and grace *(above)*. This one is in the Hôtel d'Olivary.

WALLS

There has been a dramatic shift away from the use of the plain distemper or whitewash that was common twenty years ago. Considered capable of curing all the evils of damaged and dilapidated walls, this used to be applied wherever wallpaper was not considered suitable. Now there has been a move into textured walls, rag-rolling, sponging, polished, aged, or limewashed coatings, in all of which ocher is the dominant color.

Once the ocher shades used were darker, the best known being burnt sienna. That was until the discovery of the riches of the area around Roussillon, a hilltop village in northern Luberon, near Gordes—it quickly became known as "France's answer to the Painted Desert." Near here, at Rustrel or Gargas, is the only place in France where ocher is still extracted, and it is here that Jean Faucon, the studio potter from Apt, gets his mixed earth. The proportion of iron oxide in the clay gives it the twelve distinctive shades of solid color, which do not easily bleach in the sun. That is why the painters working on exterior walls have to warn their clients not to expect the color to fade.

Ocher is a yellow sand, usually deriving its color from the presence of hydrated iron oxides; it has to be heated to turn red again. The bare rock is so hard as a result of its slow geological formation that it has to be cut out of the walls of the quarry using a bulldozer. The ore consists of 80 percent sand, and the ocher has to be separated from this. After it has been baked dry, the ocher is ground to a golden powder and packed into paper sacks for shipment. This industry flourished in the 1920s, but suffered from the arrival on the market of synthetic ochers. However, a love of the authentic won the day, and there is currently more demand than can be met for ocher pigments.

Mixing the pigments is a skilled task. Those who do so at the Conservatoire des Ocres in Roussillon explain that it is like "making a spice mixture for an exotic dish, taking saffron, cinnamon, cumin, and ginger." There are specific proportions for the mixes. A number of classes are held to teach beginners the art (mainly at Uzès and Roussillon, *see* Useful Addresses, pages 177–188). Here, in the space of a few days, one can learn to create subtle tones, make the paint, produce excellent oil paints, and of course learn the technique of texturing.

RAG-ROLLING, SPONGING, TEXTURING, AND GLAZING The effect sought in all these techniques is that of a patina that has aged over the years, and whose colors have delicately faded. Just as when antique dealers polish furniture, the main thing is to avoid that new look.

The simplest technique, but the one that produces the most disastrous results if one does not have the knack,

Stenciled friezes *(top)* are just as attractive on walls as they are on furniture.
There is not enough ocher in Roussillon to satisfy demand, now that paint and
decoration using natural pigments have become so fashionable *(facing page)*.

is rag-rolling or sponging. This is done with two matte paints of similar color, one being slight darker than the other. The first coat is put on with a roller. When it has dried completely, the second coat is applied by soaking a sponge or crumpled rag in the paint, and it is then wiped onto the walls with a circular motion. Only light pressure should be used, so that the undercoat can be seen through it. It is also important that one should not be able to see circular marks left by the sponge or cloth. This will happen if the paint is too thick or it is applied with too heavy a hand. The result is much more attractive if the second layer consists of a glaze, an oil paint. Certain craftsmen produce wonderful work, and it is easier and quicker than texturing.

To obtain the proper textured effect, several coats of paint are needed—four at least. These should be in fairly pale shades, all obtained by mixing from the same basic color. After an undercoat, which should show through until the work has been finished, a coat of oil-based paint is applied, which is the first coat of painting. It is made with linseed oil, size, turpentine, and ocher powder, or more simply by diluting the ocher in beer or water. The main thing is that the binding agent should be transparent and the coat of paint should be translucent. Then a darker coat is applied, which is worked by partly wiping it off with a cloth or sponge so that the undercoat appears irregularly. It can also be smoothed in patches with fine glasspaper to get a different effect.

For greater contrast, the third coat can be applied to the wall while it is still wet, and brushed so that the undercoat appears more intensely. Now you can see why it is a good idea to take a few days of classes, or to get craftsmen to do the work. Beginners should be aware that a textured finish can be applied over

wallpaper as long as the paper has not been vinyl treated and so is impermeable. It can also be applied to fabrics, terra-cotta, or wood. On these media, stenciled patterns can be applied, or one can paint freehand if one is skilled enough. Naturally, a different mixture should be used for each type of medium, and here again the recipes need to be learned from an expert.

There are 12 different shades of ocher, from pale yellow to black oxide, so whether used pure or mixed, the palette is almost infinite. A wall under a staircase, or a whole living room apart from the ceiling could be

Slaked lime is reserved for exteriors: Interior walls (*facing page* and *above*), are coated with whitewash tinted with ocher pigments, which mainly come from the quarries at Rustrel and Gargas in the Luberon. There is an infinite variety of shades from pale yellow ocher to dark red, and the whitewash can even be tinted azure, as in the blue room at the Château de Lourmarin.

or tiles of various different colors decorated with fruits, flowers, or landscapes, to match the frieze that surrounds them. The current fashion is for panels featuring a landscape. Water spouts from a faucet above a cobalt-blue enamel sink set in a stonework surface, while through the window can be glimpsed a field of lavender. One of Boutal's color schemes, entitled *Senteurs de Provence* (fragrances of Provence), consists of old red and Printania yellow tiles, arranged diagonally with a point at the top, surrounded by a frieze of olive branches. Basset has made friezes in relief his speciality. The terracotta peeps through the white enamel in light geometric shapes. In the bathrooms, one can wash in a world of blue and white, in which children love to recognize fish and shells depicted on the tiling.

All these smooth, uniform tiles, however beautiful, are manufactured industrially, but the famous tiles of Salernes, with their irregular surfaces, are still made by hand. They are set in thick white grout and are made in pastel shades of yellow, as if faded with time, and they are pleasant to the touch. Because they have uneven surfaces they cannot be used as table-tops or for kitchen work surfaces, but they are perfect as wall coverings.

painted in red ocher, a color scheme that can be seen in Old Nice in houses in the Genoese style. Bedrooms are often painted in pale ocher, the color of the rising sun, which is both relaxing and refreshing. This is contrasted with olive green or burnt sienna, colors repeated in the floor tiles. The color could be a little darker if the room has one of those small white marble fireplaces that are so common in all types of house, especially closer to the Italian border; the marble was quarried at Carrara.

As for kitchens, natural sienna or dark yellow ocher colors give them character, as long as the floors have pale terra-cotta or white tiles. Anyone lucky enough to have an old floor with large tiles should choose a pale ocher shade for the walls and ceiling.

Kitchen and bathroom walls become a blaze of color thanks to the multicolored earthenware tiles made by the craftsmen of Salernes such as Pierre Boutal and Pierre Basset. The walls and floors are paneled with tiles, framing small, brightly colored squares of plain tiling,

In the 18th century, the interiors of the homes of the wealthy were covered in hangings and delicately painted woodwork, like the chair *(above left)* and the panels over these doors *(facing page)*, which throw the wooden moldings and stucco curlicues into relief. The walls were covered in crushed Venetian velvet or printed cloth from Marseilles, as here in the Hôtel d'Olivary, one of the loveliest mansions in Aix-en-Provence, which can be visited by appointment.

FLOORING

Terra-cotta tiling is traditionally used to cover the floors of
houses in Provence. On this staircase *(above)*,
the risers are lined with glazed tiles. Cement tiles can be
painted *in situ* (*facing page*, showing tiles created by
the company Carocim, based at Puyricard) in order
to create bright carpets of color.

MARBLE FLOORING This does not come exclusively
from Italy. Although the floors of the Château de
Barbentane, in all their extraordinary variety, were laid
in 1774 by Neapolitan craftsmen, there were other practitioners such as Bernard Virgile Mazzetty, who came
from the Tessine in Switzerland, and settled in Avignon
in 1740. He founded a family business that lasted for
three generations, spanning a century, and Mazzetty
floors can be found throughout the region, especially in
Nîmes, Carpentras, Aix-en-Provence and Avignon. The
Mazzetty workshop employed French, Swiss, Italian,
and Spanish stonecutters, polishers, and carvers.

TERRA-COTTA The earliest tiles were of unglazed terra-
cotta and measured 12 square inches (30.5 sq. cm). They
were used for the flooring of the local Roman houses
and have never been bettered. Many homeowners haunt
architectural recyclers to get pink terra-cotta floor tiles,
worn down by just the right amount, to be laid in wide
expanses. Earthenware tiles are cosy and welcoming
with their soft patina and varied shades. Salernes is the
center of the tile-making industry, a village in which a
group of craftsmen have created the Terre de Salernes
label of authenticity. It is well worth visiting their
warehouses and stores. In addition to the classic,
indispensable hexagonal tiles—small for bedrooms,
larger for the ground floor—and unglazed terra-cotta
squares, there are the jewel-bright, glazed squares
in a rainbow of colors, which have a thousand
uses, from flooring to wallcovering, in kitchens
and bathrooms. A checkerboard of matte-glazed

black-and-white tiles, with or without splashes of color, is particularly effective against plain white walls.

In fact tiling was introduced quite recently into Provence. The Château de Lourmarin, in southern Luberon, built in the early seventeenth century, had only four rooms of brick floor tiles. The *tomette*, the brightly colored square tile typical of Provence, was "invented" by local craftsmen in the late nineteenth century, at a time when floors and staircases were mostly covered in wooden planking. This explains why, previously, the ground floors of the grand houses were covered with marble and the upper floors with parquet.

The tiled flooring industry is now flourishing, and has made extraordinary strides since the 1960s, when Jean Boutal invented a machine for manufacturing *tomettes*. In 1965 his son opened the first large factory at Port-Grimaud. Attractive tiles are also manufactured in Aubagne, Apt, and Biot.

Modern, glazed and textured tiles, terra-cotta and lava tiles from Volvic, as well as sandstone and cement tiles that are colored and stenciled with abstract, multi-colored arabesques, or shells such as the "Mer" from the Ateliers des Mousselières, illustrate the enormous range of styles, colors, and materials. There is nothing lovelier than handmade terra-cotta tiling such as the "pavés de Salernes" produced by Pierre Basset. These are compositions of shapes in various shades of faded pink, assembled in a mosaic, in a rose formation, and in tapestry patterns. There are also handmade square tiles measuring from 6–12 inches (14–30 cm), which can be laid with or without grouting to create a range of patterns in "rustic sienna." To recreate the delightful faded effect, Boutal's recipe is to mix 90 percent denatured alcohol with linseed oil, add plenty of elbow grease and "you'll get the impression that you have changed the decor."

To keep the *tomettes* in good condition, they should be polished with red wax twice year, using a soft cloth that will allow the earthenware to absorb the polish and make it stainproof. The white grouting between the tiles does not stay white for long. It can be painted with white paint, using the thinnest of artist's soft paint-brushes, though this is an exacting task. But when one opens the bedroom door and notices the soft glow of the red floor offsetting the white piqué throw over the bed, it is like a call of welcome, an invitation to rest.

Terra-cotta is the most sensual of all the construction materials used in the house; for flooring to be perfect, it should be a pleasure to run over it barefoot.

Glazed tile mosaic by Vernin of Apt *(above)*.
At Jacques Brest's studio in Salernes *(facing page)*, square tiles and *tomettes* are still molded by hand. These tiles were invented in the mid-19th century by the potters of Moustiers, who had just discovered the clay deposits at Salernes. A few examples of flooring *(overleaf),* showing well-polished *tomettes* or simply textured, polished terra-cotta tiles from Apt, friezes and square tiles from Salernes, and bright colors by Carocim.

FURNITURE AND FRAMES

In the hall, a restored couch *(radassié)*, covered in Indian-pattered cushions, stands on the small red square tiles of the entrance hall to welcome the visitor. The colors and materials harmonize perfectly, symbols of the simplicity and elegance that the people of Provence have elevated into an art of living. Expensive woods are carved, molded, bent, and chiseled, then finished with a thin coating in a delicate pastel shade. Hand-blocked fabric and handmade pottery are displayed in the reception rooms, and in the bedrooms bow-fronted chests of drawers and closets with *pieds de biche* (deer-hoof feet) are decorated with raised carvings of shells. This form of decoration even became popular in Versailles, acquiring the name of *rocaille*. In the kitchen the *manjadou* (pantry) protects provisions behind its columned door, and the loaves are safe in the deep chest used for storing bread, which is also elaborately worked as a marriage chest. Motifs include baskets of flowers, laurel branches, and musical instruments, carved in walnut for furniture and in gilt limewood for the mirrors.

The Provençal style reached its zenith in the 18th century, with ample use of flower decorations, as on the wall panels *(above)*. Painted furniture was made of pale fruitwoods, like this armoire in Jean-Jacques Bourgeois' boutique *(above* and *facing page)*.

77

A DISTINCTIVE STYLE

This little side table in the Château de Lourmarin in Vaucluse *(above)* is decorated with a technique known as *Brunswick (découpage)*, in which paper cutouts are stuck to the paint. It was very fashionable in Uzès in the 18th century. The settee in the window bay *(facing page)*, with its distinctively shaped walnut back, known as "gendarme's cap," is a late 18th-/early 19th-century version of the traditional Provençal *radassié*.

The French naval base at Toulon was the source of a distinctive Provençal style that emerged in the eighteenth century. The ships' carpenters and cabinet-makers were skilled at making balustrades and bulwarks for the poop deck, distinctive figureheads for the prow, and paneling and fitted wooden furniture for the officers' quarters. So making chests of drawers and closets to order was child's play, and an excellent way of supplementing their meager wages. The wealthy merchants of Marseilles had been in the habit of ordering their furniture from Paris, and the local aristocracy, who lived mainly in the capital, Aix-en-Provence, did not want to be outdone. They wanted their furniture to be as elegant as that at the French court. Local firms therefore began commissioning ship's carpenters to copy expensive furniture. In fact this showed that Parisian cabinet-makers had much to learn from Provence.

The woods used by these skilled woodworkers, carpenters, and cabinet-makers—as well as on a semi-industrial scale by the furniture factories of Marseilles—are always the same. They include the finest walnut, which is redder in hue in Haute-Provence, with darker markings. All the furniture was made of solid wood; veneering was almost unknown. Fruitwood furniture, made of cherry and pear, is also common. Unlike other regions, in which quality furniture uses oak supports, in Provence all the furniture used soft wood supports of pine or limewood, the latter being used to make the elaborate frames gilded with gold leaf for large mirrors. Sideboards and commodes were rarely marble-topped, except when specially commissioned.

Sculptors designed, classified, and described patterns and detailing in furniture, woodwork, mirrors, wrought and cast iron, stucco, pictures, and metalwork. Bernard Turau, known as Toro, from Toulon, was a pupil of the famous sculptor Pierre Puget (1620–1694). Toro decorated many mansions in Aix and Marseilles; he left behind numerous plates, drawings, and notebooks that were copied by all the craftsmen in the region. This is the origin of the so-called Arlesian style, often considered to be the only truly Provençal style of furniture.

A distinctive feature of the Arlesian style is that the crosspieces of closets, sideboards, and chests of drawers are all carved with a cockleshell in the center; this is flanked on both sides with swags and garlands. This style became known in Paris as *rocaille*. If the crosspieces are not decorated in this style, they may be "*décor à la soupière*" (decorated like a soup tureen), with the uprights covered in laurel leaves, roses, olive branches, or acanthus leaves. The feet are also characteristic, with their curled volutes resting on a classic plug shape. Little bureaux with a drop leaf and two drawers, and sideboards whose upper sections have sliding doors are also typical. The upper section of the sideboard is set back, allowing flatware and china to be arranged on top of the lower half. The sliding doors flank a central "tabernacle." In the Arles district, the *tamisad*, an iron mill used for sifting flour, was concealed in a lowboy. When the handle was turned, the mill separated the bran from the wheat flour. The iron frames on Arlesian furniture are thick and exposed, contributing to the decorative effect.

The cabinet-makers of Aix-en-Provence produced elegant, delicate furniture with clean lines. The chests of drawers included the deep-drawered chests on bowed legs known as a crossbow sauteuse (*sauteuse à arbalète*), whose front is made from a single piece of walnut, often decorated with thin boxwood stringing, on deer-hoof feet with thin bronze pulls.

In the Comtat Venaissin and Nîmes district, the *fustié* (the Provençal term for a woodworker) specialized in moldings, and these wide, curving decorations are carved into wood destined to become a door, a drawer, or the side panel of a piece of furniture.

The Provençal bed, known as a *litoche*, is very plain. It often consists simply of of four bedposts in the shape of pillars, and a plain headboard. This one *(facing page)* also has a footboard. Here is a return to authentic Provençal furniture. The original panels of the clothes closet *(above)* were damaged, so they have been replaced by a fine-meshed grille.

The woodworkers of Nîmes produced furniture that remained light despite its ornamentation. The commodes and closets have curving outlines, with sawn moldings that make the style a little heavier.

Haute-Provence produced a unique item of furniture, a sideboard with an added, recessed shelf, sometimes with doors. This is the ancestor of the china cabinet, an item unknown in traditional Provence furniture. The style produced at Fourques, a village at the tip of the Camargues triangle, is similar to Arlesian in style, but features arabesques and volutes gouged from the wood and called *"décor au coutar"* (snail decor). According to *Arts décoratifs en Provence*, to say that a piece of furniture was from Fourques was to mean it was plain and rustic, as the women of Arles used the word *fourcaneto* to describe a dowdy female from the poorer suburbs.

Marseilles occupies a special place in Provençal style. The most expensive woods arrived there by ship, and local customers, eager to copy Parisian styles, demanded opulent furniture. There are commodes topped with blue Turquin marble, a style that was very fashionable in the eighteenth century. Two great Marseilles furniture-makers, Louis Gouiran and Antoine Bergamin, died in 1771, and their inventory states that "there is furniture in very classic styles, in mahogany and lemonwood, solid or veneered, made of satinwood and sometimes of walnut, a large number of items in ebony, and there are stocks of wood such as rosewood, mahogany, olive wood, amaranth, lemonwood, holly, walnut, and woods from the north."

Uzès, which was once in the diocese of Avignon, and therefore of Provence, made a specialty of *arte povera*, also known as Brunswick paper, a technique used for decorating painted furniture by sticking paper cutouts on it, or having an artist paint a scene directly onto the furniture. This furniture was lined with wallpaper.

As in other regions, old tables and beds are not often used. They were made for people who were shorter, so table-tops tend to be too low and beds too short and narrow for use today. However, antique tables with attractive carved fronts—which are a rarity—can be used as consoles or dressing-tables, and if a bolster and mattress are made to order, an antique bed can be used as a very special child's bed.

Pottery, pewterware, and glassware are displayed in glass-fronted dressers and shelves (*above left* and *facing page*). These painted chairs are original but the olive green outlining the backrests has worn away.

STORAGE FURNITURE

Storage furniture is sometimes built in, such as closets under a staircase, but may still have beautifully carved doors. The living room may contain a two-piece bookcase or a corner cabinet may be fitted into the masonry. The dresser, as such, does not exist: crockery is stored in tall, closed, two-piece cabinets, or in chests topped with a matching set of shelves that are simply placed on top. To enable the top of the chest to be used for storage or as a dresser, it can be attached to the wall or placed on the ground. There are several types of shelving, including the *estagnié*, which was used for displaying pewterware; the *escudilié* for china; and the *veiriau*: the bottom part of this was for carafes and flasks, and was protected by a gallery of turned wood, and the upper shelves were for glassware.

Armoires are heavily carved and incised, with double doors. They sometimes have bulbous frontages and curving sides. Until the eighteenth century, they were finished at the top with an overhanging cornice of the shape known in French as *chapeau de gendarme*. Later the cornice is flatter, with richly carved front rails, deer-hoof feet, or volutes resting on a wedge-shaped foot to ensure stability. An expensive wardrobe would have four sculpted feet—plain back feet are considered to indicate poor quality—and would be lined with a flowered cotton print, attached by upholstery stitches concealed with braiding stuck to the surface. Such an armoire was a traditional marriage gift, and was made-to-measure by the best cabinet-maker in the area. The decoration commissioned usually included sheaves of wheat on the front rails, as symbols of prosperity for the

Polished and painted wood *(facing page)* are both traditional in Provençal furniture. The closet in pale walnut *(above)* is typical of late 18th-century Provençal style.

85

newly weds. The Arlesian marriage armoire is the most highly sought after, both for the beauty of the decoration and its emotional charge.

The most sought-after commodes are either in the "crossbow" pattern, with a slightly bowed front and central mullion, echoed in modern furniture, or those with a single or double bow-front, known as a "tomb commode." The two-drawer chests on feet, known as *sauteuses*, are a specialty of Provence. They are lighter in shape and decoration than the commodes, which are sometimes overembellished with *rocaille*. *Sauteuses* are made of fruitwood and are elegant enough to add chic

The *manjadou* was soon used for purposes other than that of a larder; this one *(above)* has unusual metalwork decoration. An 18th-century Arlesian bread box *(facing page)* in the Souleiado Museum, Tarascon, is decorated with garlands, pinnacles, turned and carved spindles. It has typical Provençal shell feet with rolled volutes on cork-shaped supports.

to a large reception room. In large items of furniture, the Transition Style is expressed mainly in the commodes with bowed feet and flat-fronted drawers, a forerunner of the classic simplicity of Louis XVI style.

Bureaux in a style known as *dos d'âne* (donkey back), halfway between a secrétaire writing-desk and a commode, have two deep drawers decorated with moldings and carvings, and were made in the plain of Arles. The interiors feature a set of miniature drawers, and often included a secret compartment.

Chests and sideboards also had double doors, and are sometimes fitted with drawers. They are often bow-fronted or with crossbow fronts. In the best quality furniture, the tops are of a single piece of wood; where the grain was palest the wood was reputed to be least sturdy, so it was placed behind the top. The structure and decoration remain unchanged in a matching upper section, which is always laid flat on the surface of the lower section. The upper piece may consist of a set of two or three drawers narrower than the one on which it rests, or a set of shelves, or even a second, taller chest, topped with a *chapeau-de-gendarme* cornice. This piece of furniture has been favored in modest country homes since Louis XIII (seventeenth century), when it featured a lozenge decoration. The following century was the heyday of Provençal style, when the sideboard with sliding doors in the so-called Arlesian style was the most representative of the fine furniture of the region.

The bread box, which was originally designed to sit on the floor, is actually more usually hung on the wall. This makes it easier to admire its elaborate carving, turned spindles, decorative metalwork and the wooden pinnacles at the top, beneath which a wheat sheaf spilled

from a basket. The *panetière* was made from a silky walnut with a close grain, carefully aged then polished regularly to preserve the patina. Originating in the plain of Arles, this once useful item spread throughout the region, doubtless due to the perfect workmanship and beauty of the walnut. Its decoration has been considered overelaborate at times, but it is reproduced in thousands of examples. Whether useful or not, it is considered an "indispensable" feature of Provençal decor.

The dough-riser is another item that long ago ceased to be a useful piece of baking equipment, but it is still one of the most heavily copied items of furniture. It is mainly used to give a rustic air to a room furnished entirely in peasant style, with exposed stonework, for instance.

The *manjadou* is a delightful larder; it looks like a small cabinet, with a lower and an upper door pierced with turned spindles to aerate the inside. Thanks to its lovely proportions, it has now graduated from the kitchen.

The sideboard with sliding doors *(facing page* and *above left* and *right*, Château d'Ansouis) is the most characteristic piece of Provençal-style furniture, especially Arlesian style, and can be found nowhere else. The top half is set back, leaving most of the top of the lower half available for storage, so it was used as a dresser-cum-sideboard. Also pictured is an 18th-century salt box *(above center)*.

ACCESSORIES AND MIRRORS

Provençal style in all its 18th-century opulence at the Château de Barbentane. Gilt, flower-patterned wood-framed mirrors *(above* and *facing page),* and a marble-topped tomb commode with brass *rocaille* decoration *(facing page).*

Small items of furniture that were used in every room in the house were also made locally, many in Aix-en-Provence, where the houses were large and the citizens wealthy, and thus able to afford these little gems. On the subject of small furnishings, there are many miniature commodes, closets, sideboards, and bread boxes that were once believed to be children's toys. In fact they are test-pieces that every apprentice had to produce as proof of his skill and his ability to earn the title of master craftsman.

The dainty drop-leaf *dos d'âne* secrétaires and sloping, single-drawer desks have a classic simplicity with their four tall legs ending in deer-hoof feet, and their sawn crosspieces. The flap, with curved edges in Louis XV style, later became rectangular, and sometimes had box-wood stringing. When the drop leaf is opened, resting on its slides, the gilt leather-covered interior is revealed, consisting of little drawers and pigeonholes.

Gaming tables and writing tables, the best of which are made of fruitwood, are in the same spirit as the secrétaires: delicate, with curved lines. The gaming tables have a little circular extension at each corner, on which to place gaming chips, and are finished with wooden beading. Writing tables are leather covered, and may have a rail around three sides.

Marble-topped, cabriolet-legged bedside tables, miniature side tables with a simple crosspiece, polished wooden chests of drawers decorated with gilding and wrought ironwork, are all indispensable items of furniture for a classic Provençal interior. They match the rest of the decor, introducing a lighter note in contrast to the heavy items of furniture in solid walnut.

Isaac Piqueret was a furniture-maker, originally from Switzerland, who lived in Avignon in the late seventeenth century. He made a speciality of small side tables with a drawer and a marquetry top, whose turned legs were linked by a worked crosspiece. Other workshops fulfilled the commissions of the wealthy inhabitants of Aix-en-Provence, Marseilles, and Avignon by producing handsome Mazarin bureaux veneered in olive wood; its strongly marked grain is well suited to this elaborate style with its gilded brass trimmings. Some of the *bastides* owned by the nobility still contain hunting tables of pale walnut or gilded wood with a marble top. These are also exceptionally fine pieces, all of which have been catalogued and are now collectors' items.

Gilding has always been in favor in Provence, and is used on picture frames, console tables, moldings, barometers and mirrors, usually on frames carved from limewood by master craftsmen. One mirror in the Hôtel de l'Europe in Avignon dates from the French Régence (1715–23), and is a classic example of all the Provençal types of decoration including "Bérain rings," a design found on Moustiers china consisting of thin rings attached to garlands. It also features fluted pilasters and grotesque masks flanked by cockleshells and garlands. The mirror is believed to be the work of Bernard Toro.

The Provençal mirrors known as "Beaucaire mirrors" were not made in Beaucaire but were sold at the big fair held annually in the town. A list of the gilders and sculptors shows most of them to be operating in Avignon and the Comtat-Venaissin, Toulon, Marseilles, Apt, Carpentras, or Nîmes. The tops, sides, and bottoms of the frames are decorated with *rocaille* and flowers, musical instruments, urns, roses, laurel wreaths, and olive branches. They have become very rare and are very valuable, especially when the mirror surface contains mercury and the frame has never needed regilding. Only the leading antique dealers sell them, and do so with a certificate of authenticity.

The guest bedroom in the house of the painter Hervé Thibault, at Les Beaumettes, in the Luberon, is mainly of baroque inspiration. The bed and the faux marble-topped bedside tables *(facing page)* are italianate, but they harmonize very well with the Provençal quilted comforter that is used in winter. A large bust of an Arlesian girl stands on a side table *(above)*; it is Souleiado's tribute to the early 20th-century painter, Léo Le Lée.

SEATING

The typical "Provençal chair" can be found everywhere. It is made of walnut or mulberry, a plentiful wood that does not rot. The back is curved and has three bowed stretchers. Sometimes, but only on painted chairs, the stretcher may be shaped like an ear of wheat, and is called *à la gerbe*. The seat is usually made of two types of rush, the weft being of sagne, a pale green reed found in the Camargue, and the top of a gold-colored reed, sometimes decorated with bands of green sagne.

In the city, upright chairs and large armchairs are made of polished walnut, carved and upholstered in silk, cotton piqué, velvet, and damask. The Provençal chair reached the height of elegance in the eighteenth century. One can find handsome painted, straight-backed armchairs of the Régence period, and armchairs of polished walnut, whose lightly grained wood with tight pores produces a wonderfully silky effect. These chairs followed the changes in style, and include high-backed Directoire chairs with open back rails to let the air circulate.

Rush-bottomed chairs are always popular in the country. The seat is often rushed with *aufo*, also known as *feuilles de Sparte*, a grass found on the banks of the River Rhône. Then there is the two-, three-, or four-seater settee, which has a rush bottom, stretchers carved with flowers, and a curved back. This is the *radassié* or *radassière*, meaning a chair on which one lazes around. The name for this light and elegant seating comes from the word *radassa*, which means lazybones. In Provence it is often used incorrectly to describe less comfortable benches that were mainly used at the table.

The Provençal chair has a fragile look, but it is very carefully constructed to include invisible reinforcements, especially in the feet *(above* and *facing page)*. A few examples of Provençal chairs *(overleaf)* show that the one unchanging feature is the width of the seat. Only the cabriolet chair, upholstered in yellow flowered cretonne, is a well-made reproduction, and is similar to the 18th-century cane chair that is shown *(top left)*.

PAINTED FURNITURE

The tradition of painted furniture is by no means new, and was not restricted to the countryside. Even in town, chairs and small closets were decorated to match the matte-painted wood paneling. Walnut was plentiful, but this noble wood was never painted.

Furniture made of solid wood that is polished and waxed, and in reality given a light coat of French polish to protect it and give it a patina, is usually of cherry-wood. It is a local tradition—and one which has always made the reputation of good cabinet-makers—to order sets of furniture for bedrooms or dining rooms. Sets were made in the eighteenth century, but this matching furniture has unfortunately long been dispersed.

It is possible, in view of the difficulty of finding an authentic Arlesian chest of drawers or a sideboard with sliding doors, to have one made. Albert Doursin of Pernes, and Jean-François Roehrig in Antibes are two of the finest contemporary cabinet-makers, and are certainly capable of producing excellent work, though they will also restore a genuine piece to its original condition. One cannot refer to their traditional pieces as "copies," nor are they reproductions, a term reserved for factory-made furniture in limited editions. These are authentic pieces, made of the same wood, using the same tools and techniques and, above all, the same skill, as in the past. It is very different from the mass-produced results from the big factories, and thanks to the connoisseurs who seek it out, they are perpetuating the presence of true Provençal furniture in our homes.

They redecorate, personalize, and recreate authentic decor in modern settings, following the fashion of sets

The *radassié* is a rush-bottomed settee first introduced in the 18th century. It is the most typical Provençal furnishing (*facing page,* in the Château de Barbentane). A small restored, painted whitewood closet and a Directoire chair with a rounded back at the Mas de Curebourg (*above*).

Painted furniture was used in plain, country interiors where the family could not afford walnut.

This attractive two-piece sideboard *(left)*, the top part of which has had mesh grilles cut into it, is unusual due to its pull-out flap which can be used to hold a few light items.

The little writing desk *(facing page)* dates from the late 18th century. It is made of hardwood and its floral decoration is hand-painted. It was restored by Francis Guaré, whose firm, Félix-Ailhaud, is situated in the heart of the old quarter of Aix-en-Provence.

of painted furniture, patinated and restored, which the company Sifas, for example, offers in 24 different shades. The wood is solid oak or beech, the latter being the favorite wood for all types of chair.

As in the case of tables, easy chairs in a home that is attempting to combine tradition and comfort should be the best that contemporary design has to offer. There should be deep wing-chairs and well-upholstered sofas,

either covered in pale linen or in a traditional Provençal fabric. The residents of Provence in earlier times would have luxuriated in today's soft furnishings. How they would have appreciated being able to snuggle under a goose-feather comforter or duvet in the freezing winter, or being able to *radasser*—laze around—on a well-sprung sofa, enjoying a refreshing siesta in the burning heat of a summer in Provence.

A few handsome examples of cabinet-making: An 18th-century
combined bureau and chest of figured, painted wood from Jean-Jacques
Bourgeois' boutique in Isle-sur-la-Sorgue *(above left)*, a fairly rare *dos
d'âne* bureau with doors *(above right)* of the same period, and a pair of
wide-backed 1950s armchairs *(facing page,* at the Mas du Pastre*)*.

CERAMICS AND GLASSWARE

Investigation of the wrecks of Roman ships that plied the coast between Sicily and Catalonia, and archeological finds in the Tyrrhenian Sea have revealed that Rome was supplied from Fréjus, southwest of Cannes, with dishes, casseroles, pots, water jugs, and amphoras. Ships visited the Estérel coast to load up with pottery containers. These were then sent to the wine-makers and the olive-oil manufacturers, and to the oyster-farmers of the Etang de Berre, who used them to transport the oysters in brine that the Romans considered such a great delicacy.

These heavy vessels were made of terra-cotta and were only glazed inside. They were the ancestors of the rustic pottery of Dieulefit and Biot. Peasants have always eaten and drunk from clay and earthenware, while the wealthy ate off solid silver, silver-gilt, and even gold. They did so at Versailles until December 14, 1689, when Louis XIV signed a "declaration regulating tableware items of gold and silver," to enable his war minister, the Marquis de Louvois, to re-equip his army. To set an example, the Sun King ordered his plate to be melted down; from then on, he only ate on china dishes. The golden age of the potters of Marseilles, Varages, and Moustiers had begun.

Earthenware is heavy and rather fragile, but it is perfect for an al fresco meal *(above)*.
The pieces in green-glazed earthenware *(facing page)* include a jar for preserves, bowls,
an 18th-century style plate, an olive pot, a water pitcher, and gadrooned salad bowls.

CERAMICS, POTTERY, TERRA-COTTA

At the Maison d'Uzès, which is a combination museum and store, Martine de Fontanes displays her love of pottery *(above* and *facing page)*. The salad bowl and plates are from Vallauris, the 19th-century pitchers from Saint-Zacharie, and the mortar is from Tornac. The magnificent kitchen in the Château des Sabran, at Ansouis, Vaucluse *(overleaf)*, with its range of table- and cookware.

Whether standing against the wall in the dining room, or in a large kitchen that can be used for family meals, the dresser might be regarded as an essential item of furniture, even if it is just a simple, modern piece made of pine. Yet in fact the dresser is not part of the Provence inventory of furniture. It is possible to find sideboards on which to display one's best china, or set soup tureens and vegetable dishes. However, it is easier to find an *estagnié*, which was used to display pewter measuring jugs, pitchers, and plates. Yet every mistress of the house had china she wanted to display, platters and dishes that she had inherited or received as gifts, or items she had acquired from antique dealers and china stores. Probably collectable china was hung on the wall in bygone days.

In every corner of the globe, shards of pottery can be found: they are as old as man's discovery of fire. They may be the remains of votive or utilitarian objects. Our distant ancestors could not yet make bowls or platters from wood, because as yet they had no sharp tools, so they worked clay with their hands, having realized that baking it in a hot fire would make it much more sturdy than merely letting it dry in the sun. That is why it is reasonable to suppose that ceramics—from the Greek word *keramon*, meaning clay—are as old as man himself.

Ceramics is the word used to describe any object made of terra-cotta, earthenware, pottery, or porcelain. Ceramics are made and sold by a potter. Nowadays the word "terra-cotta" is generally used to describe objects that are only fired once (such as flowerpots) and non-vitrified (biscuit)—meaning unglazed—ceramics.

The earliest pottery kilns have been found in Spain, but it was Faenza in Italy that lent its name to a type of ceramic known as faïence. This is made from a pure clay, protected and colored by a glaze produced in Provence. Since the seventeenth century "faïence" has been used to describe the process for making a ceramic of porous clay, coated with a glaze of lead oxide, which is made opaque by mixing it with oxide of tin. The finest pottery, which reverberates like a tuning fork when flicked with the finger, is a white paste ceramic that is fired twice, then glazed and fired again. The red or pinkish color of the clay indicates the presence of iron.

The places where the best clay deposits are found have also become large centers of production. They are Apt, Aubagne, Biot, Dieulefit, Moustiers, Salernes, Uzès, Vallauris, and Varages. Jean Faucon and Antony Pitot, potters working in Apt who get their clay from Vallauris, regret the fact that not more craftsmen exploit the local clay deposits. At Varages the Manufacture des Lauriers, founded in 1695, employs 100 people and produces five million pieces a year, making it the biggest producer of industrial and craft pottery in Provence. Like M. Offner at the nearby Faïencerie de la Belle Époque, the manufacture uses clay of diverse origins. Offner states frankly, "There's no pottery clay left. I get my supplies from a craftsman in the region who produces a pink, high-quality potting clay by mixing several clays."

At Moustiers-Sainte-Marie, however, the local clay is still very much in use. It is of an unusual composition and has a pink hue. Pottery was first made here in 1550 by the Clérissy family from Italy. The River Verdon supplies the 17 craft potters who still work here with water of exceptional purity, excellent for refining the raw material.

The potters of Moustiers were once accused of denuding the surrounding hilltops of their trees in order to fuel their kilns. Fortunately, modern electric kilns have put an end to these charges. Moustiers nestles between two steep cliffs that are linked at the top by a chain, reputedly of silver; a stream runs between the houses of the village and feeds the blue-green waters of the Verdon, with its spectacular gorges. It is hard to judge whether it is the local pottery or the lovely setting that attracts the most visitors.

The predominant colors for traditional Provençal folk pottery are sun yellow and olive green, as illustrated in this fruit bowl from Biot (*facing page*) or the little flower-patterned bowl (*above*) from Brantes.

THE TECHNIQUE Pottery has always been made in the same way. The raw clay is filtered, decanted, and dried. It is then kneaded for a long time in order to remove any air bubbles. Standard shapes are then turned on a potter's wheel, while decorative elements—fruits, grotesques, handles, and lugs—are finally stuck to the piece with slip (liquid clay).

Flatware is produced from a mold. The piece of clay is placed in a mold to give it its interior shape, and then pressed against the sides by hand. Hollowware consists of various molded parts assembled and stuck together with slip. All the pieces, including those made by the many students who flock to these potteries to learn the skill, are then dried in the sun. The pots, which are known as "greenware" at this stage, need to lose some 25 percent of the moisture they contain before the first firing. The clay will shrink as it dries, generally by about five to eight percent. The remaining moisture content will evaporate in the kiln.

Firing makes the item almost indestructible; it is stable, cannot dissolve, and can last for centuries undamaged. This characteristic makes it possible to perform a chemical analysis on old pottery. A French laboratory, the Laboratoire de Céramologie du CNRS performed such an analysis a few years ago, and discovered that many of the eighteenth-century pieces reputed to have been produced at Moustiers-Sainte-Marie in fact came from the Varages potteries.

Clay fired in a 1292°F (700°C) oven takes 40 hours to become "biscuit" (its state after the first firing and before glazing); this needs to cool for at least 24 hours. Biscuit is strong but porous. Once dried it was dipped in a bath of glaze. The glaze was made of lead oxide, silica to bleach the glaze, and tin. The relative proportions are based on the original color of the clay (the potters of Moustiers developed an excellent white glaze to conceal the pink color of their clay) and the desired result. The best potters try to avoid their glaze being too smooth and shiny—"sanitaryware glaze," as they call it at Bondil's, the largest pottery in Moustiers. Bondil uses a tin glaze that gives the pottery its semi-matte look. If the ingredients are present in the right proportions, the glaze will not crack.

Pottery that is to be decorated is then sent to the painter, who uses cobalt oxide for blue, antimony oxide for yellow, manganese for violet and brown, copper for

Jean Faucon is a potter working at Apt. At his pottery, large items *(above)* are made from a clay mixture that he excavates himself from deposits near Gargas and in Roussillon. This blue soup tureen *(facing page)* is in fine white clay decorated with a cobalt blue jasper pattern.

green, and gold dissolved in acid for the pink color known as "Cassius purple." He or she applies intricate patterns, mythical birds, garlands, birds of paradise, hot-air balloons, or roses. Many painters work in their own studio-store and have to answer questions from visitors while continuing to work so carefully and skilfully that no bird loses its feathers and no flower its petals—mistakes cannot be erased. Customers should wait to put their queries until the painter rests his or her brush. Tin-glazed pieces are then fired at high temperatures, in a small kiln that is heated to around 1832°F (1000°C).

A different technique uses lower temperatures but requires three firings. The decoration is added to the background using colors that have extract of turpentine as their base, enabling it to adhere to glaze that has already been fired. For the third firing, the kiln is heated to about 1292°F (700°C) and this fixes the decoration. This is the most expensive of the firing techniques, but it makes it possible to produce very brilliant colors. It was originally adopted to compete with the decoration of the East India Company porcelain, the classic Familles Vertes and Familles Roses that were once so fashionable in Paris.

The clay at Dieulefit has been excavated since prehistoric times, and is white or red. The glazes are always in one of three colors, green, black, and straw color, traditionally highlighted with a brown or black manganese edging. The glaze, which was known as aquifoux, was a sulfurous mixture with a high lead content, which means it could not be used for any vessel intended to contain food or drink. It is a pity that it was harmful — although the lead would disappear when fired to a temperature of 1796°F (980°C)—because the glaze was wonderfully transparent, with a mother-of-pearl effect that is so distinctively Dieulefit. Aquifoux may still be used in small quantities in the glaze, mixed with clay, silica, and oxides.

Jean Faucon of Apt still uses a very special technique, combining clays, to produce a mixture of shades. The hills of Rustrel and Gargas contain deposits of a dark red, almost violet earth, veined with brown, green, and even bluish clays. Faucon gathers clay of different shades from several places, and later mixes them.

At the Poterie Provençale in Biot, the descendants of René Augé-Laribé, whose products were first exhibited at the 1925 Exposition des Arts Décoratifs in Paris, still use the local pink-tinted white clay as the basis for making earthenware pots, glazed mainly in dark yellow, black, and green, as well as for large classic jars. Other substances are added, but—as with the details of Jean Faucon's mixtures—they are a family secret!

Like most of the local potteries, the Poterie du Soleil at Villecroze in the Haut Var perpetuates the tradition of pure shapes, such as these water jugs awaiting a waterproof glaze *(facing page)*, and this hand-turned bowl *(above)*.

DECORATION AND SHAPES

Fruit bowl by Pichon of Uzès *(above)*, identifiable
by the little flowers that decorate the strips of china made to
look like wickerwork. Plate and posset pot of the
18th century made at Moustiers *(facing page)*, probably by
Fouque, with green decoration "in the Chinese taste"
featuring grotesques.

Each pottery manufactory used to produce its own distinctive style of decoration, developed by the potters and painters. Today many potters buy plain white-glazed pottery and add their own designs, or copy classic decoration. There are three main types of decoration. Firstly there is the "authentic" style, which originated in the seventeenth and eighteenth centuries. It is often elaborate because noblemen did not want anything that looked too plain or discreet. The "classic" designs came later, and made use of flower patterns, fruits, and garlands. The "contemporary" style allows potters to give free rein to their imagination. Collectors might have a china cabinet that includes Marseilles pottery, or pieces by Veuve Perrin, or items from Moustiers, with its mythological decor. On the dresser there may be a soup tureen of mixed clay by Jean Faucon, and the tableware may be rustic style earthenware from Dieulefit or Biot, whose only decoration is a single stripe. Octagonal plates in seventeenth-century style from Apt or Dieulefit are edged with a simple groove and sometimes with raised beading. Eighteenth-century plates had gadroons and cutaway edges, edged with an ocher, green, or blue stripe.

AUTHENTIC STYLE As soon as the demand for china began, Moustiers outdid Marseilles, Montpellier, and Varages, its rivals. Pierre Clérissy, who by 1679 was known as a "master potter," surrounded himself with painters; within twenty years they had made the village famous. This was the era of decoration known as *à la Berain*, which consisted of hunting scenes and coats of

116

arms taken from collections of the work of Florentine engraver Antonio Tempesta (1555–1630). Birds, flowers, and figures were incised into the glaze. The decoration was consistently blue, but a few touches of ocher would later be added, and eventually it became multicolored.

The winter of 1709 was so cold that even the River Seine froze over, causing an unprecedented famine. The king insisted on continuing French involvement in the War of the Spanish Succession (1701–14), however. So the last gold and silver plate was melted down and the fashion for china reached its height. Clérissy, the potter from Moustiers, even opened a store in Paris. In order to compete with porcelain, earthenware pottery adopted Chinese patterns, then birds and grotesque figures, of the type that can be seen in frescoes in Italian Renaissance villas. The decor was in a single color, usually blue, olive green, or yellow, or sometimes in two colors. There are also mythological decorations surrounded by garlands of flowers known as the "potato flower pattern," and later "solanum flower pattern;" this was so popular that it was even copied in China.

French victory at the battle of Fontenoy in 1745 inspired decoration consisting of patriotic flags and trophies; the French Revolution, the establishment of the French Empire, and important scientific discoveries of the period were also recorded by the potters. Types of china had to be matched to the taste of the buyers. Like Richelieu, Madame de Pompadour favored Moustiers pottery. So the potters had plenty of encouragement.

In Marseilles, the Spanish were the leading producers of pottery, and the decoration consisted mostly of flower patterns. It was distinctive in that the background glaze was yellow, a sunny ocher, rather than white.

In the 1750s, all the French manufactories produced patterns featuring lifelike flowers, Strasbourg producing the best pieces. The Varages flower garlands and the roses painted by the Ferrat brothers at Moustiers were the most popular patterns. In Marseilles, Veuve Perrin's birds and insects depicted in relief were added to the fruits and flowers. Fish and other marine creatures were used in baroque fashion, to decorate a wine-cooler, for example. Today, while at Moustiers, Varages, and Dieulefit the antique patterns are reproduced, in Marseilles only Gilberte Figuières reproduces eighteenth-century Marseilles pottery, using the original materials, low-firing technique, and decoration. Demand is so great, however, that the floral patterns have had to be simplified.

Four 18th-century pieces: Flower garlands became the symbol of Varages *(top left)*; Moustiers offset the elaborate nature of its decoration by using shades of green, "Chinese style" *(top right* and *bottom left)*; and multicolored grotesques adorn tin-glazed earthenware fired at low temperatures *(bottom right)*. The stenciled kitchenware *(above)* is 19th-century.

THE CLASSICS Instantly recognizable and never out of fashion, this type of decoration can be described, without being derogatory, as universally acceptable. While a pierced-rim cake plate by Veuve Perrin, in the Uzès style, would be a little too elaborate for the modern table, there is nothing more delightful and timeless than the little fruits produced by Sicard of Aubagne, which look like rosebuds or cherries, but are in fact rose hips. Their scarlet color and tiny green leaves stand out against the bright yellow background. Most of the decoration is stamped or sponged on, a mass-production technique that is slightly more delicate than transfer-printing. There is a fairly plain central motif, with a border consisting of a thin garland. This should satisfy those who do not like unpatterned china.

Classic designs that never go out of style include a simple line of colored glaze on the rim of plain or decorated plates and hollowware, and the groove—which may also be edged with beading—that decorated plain china in the seventeenth and eighteenth centuries, especially the octagonal plates of Apt and Dieulefit.

CONTEMPORARY CHINA: FUTURE CLASSICS AND NEW IDEAS Some potters would not abandon traditional techniques for anything. These include Georges E. Gerre of Moustiers, who only uses tin glaze, and only paints eighteenth-century patterns. Others create designs in the spirit of the age, such as the *Cabanon* series of pottery created in Varages by the Manufacture des Lauriers. The Souleiado stores sell china using *boutis* patterns, such as the Fleur d'Arles. In Varages, primitive flowers are painted on fine china, and Marcelle et Jeanine Cesana decorate their porcelain with oriental flower patterns. These twin sisters, born at Roubaix in 1930, used to be Limoges porcelain painters, but when the factory closed they moved south to Barjols, near Varages, and have worked for the Manufacture des Lauriers since 1965. Their work is likely to become classic. The little bowls made by the Poterie Provençale at Biot reproduce Art Deco designs, such as stylized rosettes. The slightly transparent glaze that reveals the pink of the clay, a speciality of Offner at Varages, is particularly attractive.

The Atelier Soleil at Moustiers has developed a glaze, mottled with gray, highlighted by bright pink. This pottery also produces tea and coffee services whose handles are butterflies with spread wings. Terre et Provence is a special case. This pottery at Dieulefit is extraordinarily popular and its work can be found in stores in many cities. It is tough yet countrified, glazed pottery in traditional shapes, decorated with olives, fruits and flowers, or geometric friezes that are resolutely modern. This is the sort of china that should be used for eating outdoors, an equivalent of the stoneware that is favored in other regions of France.

Clay bowls of a single color with multicolored jasper glaze decoration *(above)*. Late 19th-century hollowware in mixed clays from Apt *(facing page)*, with typically fussy design. Modern glazed terra-cotta bowls from Biot, Salernes, Villecroze, and Dieulefit *(overleaf)*, including platters, *tians*, mixed clay flask, pestle and mortar, dishes, vinegar pot, and a melon dish.

TABLEWARE

A 19th-century Vallauris faïence dish *(above)*. The pearly sheen of the enamel indicates that this Provençal Louis XVI-style *tourterelle* service *(facing page)* is made at Poët-Laval, near Dieulefit, in the département of Drôme. The square dishes, photographed at the Maison d'Uzès, are inspired by 1930s patterns.

Every Provençal home ought to have a set of faïence tableware to enhance the brightly colored dishes of the region. I had long wanted such a service, so I asked Antony Pitot to make one for me. I discovered this fine artist (who is loquacious when one gets him on his own) when I saw some of the pieces made by him that his sisters displayed in their Souleiado store in Apt. This gave me the opportunity to make a number of visits to his dry-stone house, surrounded by flowers, located on the road from Apt to Carpentras. Leaving the car under the trees, one climbs a narrow flight of stairs to reach the little display room. Each time I visited him, I admired an old Sicard plate that was yellow with a lovely rose-hip pattern, but he would never sell it to me. Antony Pitot completed my service: needless to say, it is such a rare pleasure to be able to see a piece that has been potted and glazed especially for you.

Complete dinner services are not actually in great demand. Offner of Varages only makes about four or five a year, all of them commissioned, as wedding presents. At Dieulefit, Moustiers, and Biot, customers tend to buy sets of plates or a piece of hollowware. A complete service can be built up gradually, piece by piece, because the potter continues to produce the same designs.

It is a good idea to avoid choosing muted or unusual colors such as blue-black or lavender, on which—apart from some desserts or cheeses—food will not look particularly appetizing. I prefer to stick to primary colors, such as yellow, which can be found in almost every shade from ocher, sunshine yellow, to almost brown. It enhances the look of stews, civet of hare, fish, and

ratatouille, while green is perfect for serving tomatoes, melons, filled zucchini, barbecued food, and green salad.

Faïence is fairly fragile, unfortunately, and even a slight shock can do it irreparable damage. It is this disadvantage that has made it less popular than porcelain, which is so much tougher, or glazed terra-cotta, which is more primitive looking but lasts much longer. But faïence has other great advantages: the cream color of the paste where it is revealed beneath the glaze and the sensual touch of the piece are incomparable. The edge of the plates are never thin and sharp, as in porcelain, the hollowware is never angular, and the bowls, which fit into the palm of the hand like a morning kiss, are what makes faïence pottery so much better than the rest. Just looking at it reveals its superiority: it glitters and glows with reflections that bounce off the grooves in octagonal plates, off the lugs of the soup bowls, and off the knobs and the fruit shapes on the tureen lids.

I prefer plain faïence for plates, perhaps because I like country cooking, and a panful of clams looks incongruous against a pattern of eighteenth-century grotesques. Only bright colors are really suited to Provençal tableware for informal dinners. One can match muted colors of china to certain fabrics, but this will always spoil the look of the food on the plate.

Factory-made faïence, such as that from the Manufacture des Lauriers, is tougher than studio pottery, but it is still elegant due to the clay, the glaze, and the subtle decoration. It is inexpensive, available in department stores, hardware stores, and decorator stores. It brightens the table, especially if one shape of plate is used in various colors. A more elegant note can be added to the service if the bowls, serving platters, and hors-d'oeuvres dishes are of expensive faïence, as these pieces will be subjected to less wear and tear than the other dishes.

"Apartment faïence" is the name given to those pieces of china that are displayed between courses, but are never actually eaten from, such as soup tureens, winecoolers, and fruit bowls, of which the finest, if Moustiers will forgive me, are from Marseilles.

All the hollowware produced by Jean Faucon, whether marbled or not, is of museum quality. I am thinking in particular of the wonderful covers for vegetable tureens, whose handles consist of a vine branch covered in bunches of grapes, the little marbled cups with a white edge and handle, the woven or pierced baskets in Uzès style, the oil-flasks and dessert serving bowls. Candy boxes, pill boxes, and snuff boxes were usually reserved for bedrooms, as were the pitchers and basins used for washing.

The potters of Varages, in the département of Var, continue to make fine white faïence in traditional 18th-century shapes. Their work includes dishes and platters with raised decoration of fruits, flowers, or masks (*above* and *facing page*). In her studio at La-Colle-sur-Loup, Jacqueline Morabito designs fine faïence tableware in traditional or ultra-modern styles, all in five or six shades of white, that is produced in Vallauris and at Pichon in Uzès.

POTTERY FOR THE KITCHEN

One item that should always be made of faïence is the *tian*. This is a deep dish, with or without a lid, that is placed in the oven. The tougher and heavier the clay, the more tasty the dishes cooked in it. All the summer vegetables—zucchini, eggplant—are cooked in a *tian*, as are meats in sauce that need reheating.

Then come the olive pots and pitchers. The latter are often believed to be purely for keeping water cool, but when they were made of terra-cotta and only enameled on the inside, they were attached in bunches to the neck of the pedlar's donkey and were used to hold olive oil, which does not like light or heat. There are also jugs, oil-flasks, ovenproof roasting pans and stewpots made of fireproof pottery, in which civet of hare can simmer over the embers; there are salt boxes and flour boxes, with lids of polished walnut or olive wood in their "tourist" versions. Some have spoons or several compartments, and in the antique version produced at Dieulefit they are decorated with grotesque masks.

Mortars were used to pound garlic, which was then added to the *rouille*, a spicy rust-red sauce, to produce the fragrant paste for *soupe au pistou*; the best examples of these mortars are made from marble rather than faïence. Olive wood is now also fashionable for mortars, as it is for making salad bowls and slotted spoons for serving olives. Antique examples of the vinegar pot can still be found in Apt faïence at the Isle-sur-la-Sorgue; modern ones are made of colored faïence, mainly yellow, but stoneware is more suitable for vinegar. Every kitchen has holders for kitchen utensils in glazed terra-cotta: the prettiest are decorated with slip and are made in Italy, but they go very well with our kitchenware.

Vallauris is famous for its cookware; roof tiles and bricks have been made there since the eleventh century. When the village was populated by the Genoese in the sixteenth century, kitchenware became the local industry. Feluccas and galleons would stop at Golfe-Juan to load up with pots, pans, and casseroles of every type. They were bound for North Africa, Italy, and Spain. The revival of Vallauris began in the 1920s, when Placide Saltalamacchia, an Italian potter and his wife, opened a kitchen pottery studio that is still going today.

Glazed earthenware vessels on an old kitchen sink (*above*): *tians*, mixing bowls, stewpots, pans and strainers, vases and pitchers. These are all being produced today in Salernes. Water jugs, kitchenware, fondu dishes and *tians*, and a sieve *(facing page)* are made of earthenware fired at a very high temperature, which makes them ovenproof. The preserves jars *(facing page, bottom left)* are glazed inside, as were the ancient amphoras used for shipping wine and oil.

GLASSWARE

There is only one glass-making center in Provence—Biot. But the village contains so many glassblowers and glassware designers that the classic shapes and colors they use are constantly being enriched with new ideas. The setting is delightful, a hilltop village overlooking pine-covered hills and the noisy gaiety of Antibes. From here the inhabitants, in their old houses with tiny windows that seem to rise straight out of the rocks, can watch the sea change color with the seasons, and see the ships sail by noiselessly, as if in a silent movie. All the beauty of the Côte d'Azur is there without the cacophony; just the buzz of the cicadas, what joy!

The glassmaking studios all lie between Antibes and the village. Once past Marineland, just watch for the signboards, because they are everywhere. In the studios fascinated visitors can watch the glow of the kilns and the puffed cheeks of the glassblowers, sweat running down their faces, as they manipulate the translucent glowing balls of glass. Among the objects produced will be drinking glasses, water pitchers with a section for ice-cubes, ice buckets, salad bowls, sundae glasses, serving bowls, oil bottles, carafes, candle-holders, bud vases, candy dishes, and perfume sprays.

One cannot but enjoy drinking from the stemmed glasses produced in Biot, in which bubbles are imprisoned in a substance that varies in color from bluish-gray, almost white, through cobalt blue. Glassware has many colors in Biot—pink, lavender blue, saffron yellow. True, it is not the ideal wineglass for appreciating the color of a wine, but there are decanters in an almost transparent glass that allow the wine to decant slowly from the

funnel along the sides of the high neck before dropping into the bulbous body. The hollowware—bowls, vases, and pitchers—is also delightful. An individual piece of Biot glassware stamps the decor as belonging to Provence, and marks its faithfulness to the territory.

Contemporary Souleiado porcelain reproduces the Arlesian girls *(facing page)*, as depicted in the paintings of Léo Le Lée, an early 20th-century painter who loved the Arles district and the Camargue. The most suitable china for a vinegar pot is sandstone. This oil-flask in Biot glass *(above)* reproduces an antique Etruscan shape.

TRADITIONAL FABRICS

The story of Provençal fabrics begins in the port of Marseilles, where ships arrived from the Levant in the days of the Ottoman Empire, discharging huge bales of cloth. The imported fabrics included Egyptian cotton, Syrian cloth, and delicate muslins from India, printed in paisley designs or flower patterns. These oriental fabrics and designs became enormously popular in Provence, which turned them into one of its greatest assets. No sooner had the fabrics crossed the threshold of the Provençal home than they were turned into patterned mattresses and quilts, upholstery, frills, and furbelows. French windows were curtained in a single sheet of fluttering muslin, brilliant cloths adorned the tables, and brightly colored, well-padded cushions were added to armchairs. Beds were covered in plain silk bedspreads, or elaborately quilted comforters, decorated with rose or lilac patterns. Finally, there was the cradle, which was swathed in a pure white muslin of the finest weave, soft and delicate as a spider's web so as not to scratch the delicate skin of a baby, the quintessence of the embroideress's skill.

These brightly patterned cottons are called *indienne*, perpetuating the colors and patterns imported from India in the late 17th century. An antique *boutis (above)*, made from different fabrics, like the quilted counterpane *(facing page)* in the Michel Biehn collection.

ANTIQUE FABRICS

Balthazar de Puget redecorated the Château de Barbentane
in the Italian taste in the late 18th century. Hence the use of
wallpaper, which is very rare in Provence, in floral patterns
to match the cretonnes and percales *(above* and *facing page)*,
which were woven and made up locally.

The history of fabric in Provence is a cosmopolitan
one. It was a Jew, one of those banished from
Andalusia in 1497 as part of the Expulsion from Spain,
who began manufacturing silken cloth in Marseilles.
The Spaniards came to the city to teach the art of velvet
weaving, and the Venetians that of making scarlet
blankets. The Armenians shared their techniques for
improving the quality of prints. Marseilles exported
American cochineal to Constantinople, and Languedoc
woolen cloth, as well as gold and silver cloth, to the
Portuguese, Italians, and Persians. It was an extremely
lively commercial center. So it is hardly surprising that
the fabrics used to decorate Provençal homes arrived in
the late seventeenth century from the Near East. They
often bore the name of the cities of their manufacture,
and these have been retained, though in rather distorted
form, as tarlatan, organdie, calico, nansouk, malle molle,
peking, bayadère, taffeta, chintz, mohair, and so on.

Most of these were cotton fabrics, processed in
various ways depending on the provenance. The printed
muslins worn by Indian women can be found all over
the subcontinent; very fine white percale was imported
from Pondichery, a French colony in India, as were the
prints and the painted, embroidered, warp-dyed, and
striped fabrics. Two types of pattern were typical,
regardless of the fabric. The first were the Persian patterns, known in the English-speaking world as paisley,
designs of Arab origin represented on Persian carpets;
the second were the Indian patterns, mainly taken from
the illustrations in the herbals brought to the Moghul
court by the Jesuits. This explains the absence of living

134

creatures and landscapes; the only tree depicted on antique Provençal fabrics was the Tree of Life.

Europeans loved these fabrics, whose predominant colors were violet, every shade of pink, bright blue, and turmeric yellow—and they never faded. The French court was so enthusiastic about them that at the first performance of Molière's comedy, *Le Bourgeois Gentilhomme*, on October 14, 1670, Molière was wrapped entirely in Indian cloth when playing the Grand Turk.

These cottons, known in French as *indiennes*, were made into curtains, pillows, valances, bed-hangings, and drapes, and used to upholster armchairs and line clothes closets. But since this merchandise was imported it was very costly, and protectionist measures soon banned its importation anyway. The way was clear to developing locally made fabrics of the same type. At first, the technique was very hit-and-miss; it took nearly a century for the textile workers of Provence to acquire the skills for making these prints. They learned their craft through industrial espionage. In 1734, Antoine de Beaulieu sailed for Pondichéry, at the expense of the French Compagnie des Indes. His mission was to bring back the recipe for the dyes and the secrets of this indelible fabric printing. He discovered that the colors were made permanent through the use of mordants, salts that fixed them and, when thickened with gum arabic, impregnated the cloth and made the dye insoluble in water.

Marseilles became famous for its painted cloth. Tapestries of cotonine (a mixture of linen and cotton) painted with tempera decorated the walls of the *bastides* and châteaux of the région. Designs included golden medallions on a cream background, greenery, and yellow and blue monochrome landscapes. Marseilles

cloth, cotton printed with Indian patterns, made great use of red, a dye brought from Andrianople to Marseilles by the Armenians. The background color was usually cream or cobalt blue. Cloth-dyers opened workshops in Marseilles, Aix-en-Provence, Avignon, Nîmes, Orange, Tarascon, Toulon, and in the Drôme, and rented the large fields they needed for drying the cloth that had been dyed with madder, a dark red pigment.

The patterns were adapted to a new, Provençal style. In addition to the flowers, designers added fragrant herbs, and branches of olives and grapes, small bouquets, tiny fruits, and bees. Indian pink was replaced by less strident colors, such as the pale green of the olive

The big textile firms introduce new patterns by combining designs or changing color schemes to match changing tastes. They carry a huge range in their reserve stock, such as this rose-motif counterpane *(above)*, and this 19th-century quilting with a lilac pattern by Souleiado *(facing page)*.

leaf, or stronger colors such as deep bronze. These were printed on Egyptian percale, an excellent material for making washable *indiennes* with a white or colored background, including a deep blue from Antioch and red from Smyrna.

Other influences were introduced in the nineteenth century. First came the Directoire, with its straight lines, stripes broken with flowers, checks, ovals, and various shades of lavender; then the Empire, with its polka dots. The patterns were always tiny. Napoleon loved them and gave many checker-patterned fabrics to the Empress Josephine. At the Jourdan workshops at Tarascon, now the Souleiado factory, there are piles of pearwood textile printing blocks in which these patterns are carved. Despite the ravages of the Industrial Revolution, when many of the blocks were burned, 40,000 remain, and they are still used to make fabric to order, when a collector wants cloth printed in the traditional way.

Les Olivades opened at Saint-Étienne-du-Grès in 1818, at the height of the Romantic period. Its fabric colors included faded ocher, an almost silvery green (the eternal search for the color of the olive leaf), and dull pinks.

Visits to the Maison Biehn at Isle-sur-la-Sorgue, the Château-Gombert in Marseilles, and other collections, reveal that, faithful to the original designs, Provençal craftsmen never introduced human figures, animals, or landscapes into their patterns. There might be the occasional bird, and a few mythological scenes in Toile-de-Jouy style, as in certain designs recently revived by Les Olivades. Lavender was not one of the herbs depicted in patterns because its cultivation is of recent date. The representations were always stylized, a trend that became stronger with the advent of modernism.

The printing and research workshop at the Souleiado museum in Tarascon (*above* and *facing page*). The colors and patterns are developed on the basis of the color charts and the thousands of woodcut pattern blocks that have been carefully preserved. A valuable heritage of quilts and *boutis* has survived, as can be seen in these 19th-century pieces (*overleaf*). Only the fabrics on page 141 (*top left*) are modern.

QUILTING AND FURNISHING FABRICS

Boutis fabrics are one of the finest products of Provence;
looking at them against the light *(above)*,
emphasizes their delicacy. They should be made
from a very fine, tightly woven percale. A wedding *boutis*
(facing page) by Le Rideau de Paris, decorated with palmetto
leaves, flowers, and beads.

Quilted fabrics originate from Central Asia, where the winters are bitterly cold and the summers scorching hot. Tadjik tribesmen on their donkeys still wear hand-quilted kaftans, whose shabby blue exterior with their pink frogging hide a bright, flower-patterned quilted lining to protect them from the cold.

In Provence the various ways in which the fabrics were used produced wonderful results. Whether quilted, or used as upholstery fabric or for furnishings (*boutis*), they were all very sought after by collectors.

Quilts are made in cloth with large patterns, as well as in plain silks, taffeta, moirés, and brocades. The upper surface would be created in an expensive, patterned fabric, since this would be the side on view, with mattress ticking in striped or plain hemp or silk padding for the underside, and a layer of silk or cotton wadding in between. Sometimes there is a central square of brightly colored fabric, contrasting with a wide border in a different fabric. A profusion of different quilting motifs added their designs to those of the cloth.

When plain fabrics, usually silk, are quilted, the patterns are traditionally elaborate, not leaving a square inch undecorated, and they are often thrown into relief by stumpwork, the origin of the *boutis*.

Matelassage is a simpler form of quilting, a technique typical of Marseilles, which is used on fragile fabrics that would not withstand heavy quilting. It is also used on fabrics that are so heavily patterned that fancy stitching would not look attractive on them.

If it is made entirely of silk, a quilted comforter measuring 40 square inches will weigh no more than

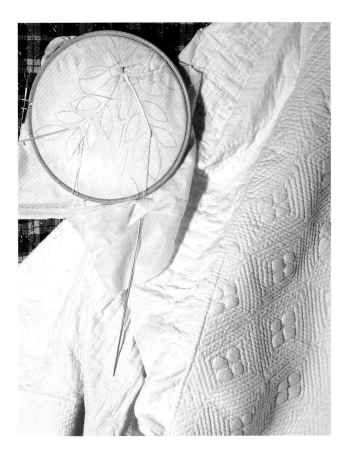

Winter is when Provençal beds can be used to display rich fabrics and warm quilting. Lovely collections of *boutis* are on show all over the region. A *boutis* bedspread *(facing page)* by Le Rideau de Paris, a Souleiado example *(left)*, and quilting *(below)* from the private collection of the antique dealer Jean-Jacques Bourgeois.

eight ounces (250 grams per square meter); if it were made of cotton or wool and padded with cotton in the normal way, it would weigh six times more.

Boutis, also known as *broderie emboutie*, is one of the most beautiful of folk arts. The white fabrics are of the finest percale, which should be looked after with great care, since the quality of the fabric is irreplaceable. Small ones were made for cradles to be given as gifts, but they needed to be started even before the mother-to-be was betrothed, because each took more than a thousand hours to make. *Boutis* are prepared in the same way as quilting. Once the two thicknesses of fabric and their intermediate wadding have been assembled, the

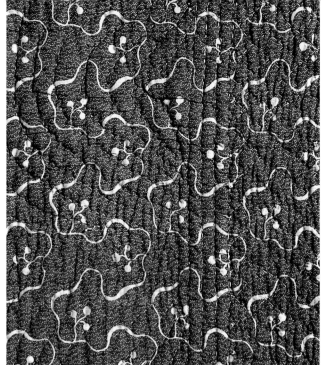

A quilted counterpane by Souleiado *(top right)*, and
recreations by Le Rideau de Paris using patterns of
hortensias and anemones *(above)*. Quilted throws and
counterpanes are usually covered in printed fabric on the
top or front and plain fabric on the underside or back, as in
this child's quilted comforter with its lovely convolvulus
pattern *(facing page)*, which is by Florence Maeght.

patterns are traced, pricked by hand in double outline,
before the thick cotton thread, the *boutis*, is threaded
with a bodkin between the pricked out areas to throw
them into relief. The quilting patterns cover the whole
fabric in a riot of curlicues, palmetto leaves, artichokes,
or geometric shapes. The result is magnificent, all the
more astonishing if one examines it against the light.

The work is so meticulous, so delicate, and has
become so rare that Provençal *boutis* are now collectors'
items, and the term may one day become a registered
label or an appellation of origin. It is a pity that many
merchants, and even manufacturers such as Valdrôme,
attach the magic word *boutis* to plain quilted coverlets,
many of which are mass-produced in India.

The elaborate quilting technique used to produce a
boutis can now be learned from books, through societies
and associations, and even on the initiative of a few dry
goods stores that bring in an expert on one afternoon a
week during the winter months to teach the craft to a
group of embroiderers and help them with their work.
A few winter and spring courses are held in Provence,
on which the local embroidery techniques are taught in
French and in foreign languages.

NEW FABRICS

featherlight white muslin, or in ocher cotton or flower-patterned lavender. They are made into counterpanes and comforters, table mats, and cushions. Unquilted patterned fabrics use the same color scheme of ocher, red, olive green, and sky blue, and are woven in percale, piqué, linen, and cretonne to decorate the house and to brighten plain fabrics with patterned trim. The great Provençal weavers of today are Souleiado, Les Olivades, Valdrôme, and Les Indiennes de Nîmes, all of whom produce classic patterned *indiennes*. Examples are Valdrôme's piqué printed with a rose trellis pattern on a white background, and the Indian lilac pattern by Les Olivades.

The big manufacturers have produced variations in the materials and designs that are better suited to modern life. They include plasticized tablecloths for kitchens and outdoor eating, and quilted table mats with matching napkins. There are new ideas in each collection: Souleiado has produced porcelain to match its fabrics with their burnt-sienna background. Today's art consists in harmonizing the most disparate patterns. Les Olivades combines flower patterns with stripes and squares that are printed or jacquard woven in shades of a single color. Patterns include a series of Toile-de-Jouy-style prints in shades of blue, ocher, or almond green, and Marseilles piqué decorated with the lozenge-shaped pattern known as a calisson, as well as checks and stripes. These combinations are surprising, but they work. Jean-François Boudin, who runs Les Olivades with his wife Françoise, repeats a Provençal saying: "*Es pas beù ço qu'es beù, es beù ço qu'agrado.*" ("Beautiful is not beautiful; that which is pleasing is beautiful.")

Provençal fabric designs are enjoying a huge comeback, after falling out of favor from the 1950s to the 1970s. They are popular throughout the world, but especially in the United States, where the elaborate French quilting technique, which gave rise to American quilts, is particularly admired. Provençal-style fabric is now printed in many countries, wherever cotton is grown. Hand-quilted coverlets are manufactured in India in

Small-patterned fabrics, such as these *(above)* from Souleiado using flowered or stylized motifs in one or more colors, are among the most popular of modern Provençal styles. Bright printed fabrics, such as this Jacqueline Carcassonne design *(right),* provide the perfect background to a heavily laden table set for a summer meal outdoors.

The major manufacturers offer traditional prints that are plasticized to make them suitable
for informal meals. These *(facing page right)* are Souleiado fabrics. The patterns are
available in every colorway, so different prints can be combined. The Jean-Jacques
Bourgeois armchair *(above)* is covered in the famous "Cupid" pattern by Les Olivades.

IN THE GARDEN

The garden is an important part of the Provençal home. Houses are south facing, so even in January, if the day is sunny, one can sit outside on a bench next to a wall that is slightly warm. It is also possible, on days without wind, to breakfast in the sun at the stone table that is always there and impervious to bad weather. When summer comes, there is plenty of shade, often from plane trees. Armchairs and garden furniture are brought out, the geraniums and nasturtiums provide cascades of bright color, and the orange and lemon trees planted in big pots decorate the terrace. As much time as possible is spent outdoors, for meals, siestas, and special occasions. The only sounds are the buzzing of the bees in the lavender bushes and the splash of a fountain. It is the season for outdoor eating at colorful tables, enjoying pitchers of ice-cold rosé wine, and using brightly colored flatware matched with cotton napkins. Barefoot on the terracotta tiles, one surveys the garden and says to oneself that the geraniums need deadheading and the begonia, which has spread too quickly, needs cutting back, "maybe today, or if not then maybe tomorrow."

Calades are mosaics in stone, expanses of river pebbles embedded in mortar. The contrasting colors of the pebbles make them into a decorative feature. This one *(above right* and *facing page)* is in the garden at Val Joanis in Pertuis, in the Vaucluse.

THE TERRACE

Shade is a priority near the house. The terrace of the
Château d'Ansouis *(above)* with its row of stone vases and
the terrace of the Mas Dargent in Saint-Rémy *(facing page)*.

This is one of the essential features of a house in the
country. Whether a château, *bastide*, *mas*, or townhouse, every house has this transitional space between
the rather private interior and the garden. The terrace
is laid out in front of the building, and is used as an
extension of the living quarters as soon as the weather
permits. It is a sort of summer living room, shady,
paved, flowery, decorated, and carefully laid out; a kind
of ante-chamber to the house. It completes the image
provided by the façades, and is a foretaste of the style
of the interior, its harmony and authenticity.

A *mas* usually has a driveway leading to it from one
side, a dirt road lined with trees, while *bastides* have
handsome avenues leading up to them at right angles
to the main entrance. The grounds of the Château de
Florans, at which the La Roque-d'Anthéron Piano
Festival is held, is an extreme example, with its double
row of plane trees with a grassy expanse in between. A
row of sequoias has been planted at right angles to the
drive, to offset the oval ornamental pond and the flight
of steps leading to the terrace.

In humbler homes, which are often built on slightly
raised ground to allow rainwater to drain away, a low
wall separates the terrace from the garden, which is on
a slightly lower level. The garden is a place for walking
through and around, for growing flowers and vegetables. It has ornamental ponds, statues, and paths edged
with lavender. There may be flowerbeds and boxwood
topiary work inherited from the Renaissance, of which
there are extraordinary examples at the Château
d'Ansouis near Cucuron, in the southern Luberon.

If the garden is on a hillside, an embankment built of stone (*restanque*) may border the terrace. It will be topped with planters containing flowers or shrubs, separating it from the olive trees with their changing colors, or the summer opulence of the fruit trees.

Like the house, the terrace is more sophisticated than it first appears. Banks of flowers blooming against the frontage; the large table under a plane tree; the chairs and stone benches placed to take advantage of the winter sun and the summer shade; the terra-cotta vases containing brilliantly colored geraniums; the citrus trees with their dark green, shiny leaves; the trellis covered with flowering vines: all these elements seem to have been thrown together by accident—or to have been there for ever. The paving is an important feature, once again created by the skill of the local craftsmen.

Trellises, awnings, and arbors provide shady seating areas at the home of landscape artist Dingwall Maine *(above left)*, and at the Mas Dargent *(above right)*. The garden of a guesthouse in Avignon *(facing page)*, with its contrasts between light and shade.

PAVING

Rows of pebbles or cobblestones are laid beside façades or in avenues to enable rainwater to run off quickly, as here at Val Joanis *(above)*. A terrace *(facing page)* consisting of rows of paving stones, laid edge-to-edge without mortar.

Architects are required to ensure that the paving used for the terrace adjoining the house harmonizes with the building itself. In the handsome eighteenth-century *bastides*, especially those used as wineries where the ground floor is used exclusively for storing wine, as at the Château de Mesclances at La Crau in the Var, the terrace is a large area in proportion to the dimensions of the façade, covering the entire width of the building. The same design is used for the Mediterranean villas; these are built on piles, so the ground floor is unoccupied. The terraces here are paved with large terra-cotta or stoneware tiles, or in textured, mossy, flattened cobblestones. The faded colors are well-matched to the smooth plaster and ornamentation of the façade. The terrace is often separated from the garden by a stone balustrade, and is shaded by the frontage of the house. It often opens onto a large central stone flight of steps leading to clumps of trees and a water feature. This leads to an avenue of plane trees, which links the main road, the vineyard, the cellars, and the residence.

In the *mas* and village houses, whose secret gardens are invisible from the street, the terrace has an important role to play. The paving is often very intricate, and can be a genuine work of art. There is often an avenue of flat stones, laid in geometric patterns, or fieldstone, as at the Serre de La Madone, Menton. All around the house, and along the width of the façade, there is a paved area designed mainly to allow water to run off quickly, since in Provence it rains in short, heavy bursts.

Two attractive paving techniques are used for paths or avenues in level gardens. *Calpinage* is the name given

to brickwork, laid on edge and often in a herringbone pattern like a parquet floor. Over the years it acquires a rich flora of grasses and moss, which grow in the gaps between the bricks. The pale green blends with the pink of the terra-cotta in a combination of muted tones. Narrow channels, the same depth as the bricks used, efficiently drain the rainwater away.

Calades, an Italian feature, consist of expanses of river pebbles in contrasting colors, ranging from black to white, assembled on the spot in curving and round patterns, and fixed in place by packed earth covered in a thin screed of mortar. They are also used in the garden itself to mark the paths that wind between low boxwood hedges, as at the Château d'Ansouis. These *calades* also decorate the forecourts of many major buildings in Provence, such as that of the Musée de l'Annonciade in Saint-Tropez and in the old quarter of Nice. They may be made of colored stones or marble. François Dovillez, a specialist designer of *calades*, makes squares measuring 16–20 inches (40–50 cm) per side, made up of Var pebbles attached to slabs, so that various designs can be produced quickly and easily.

Beyond the avenue and the sidewalk, the terrace is simply covered in grass, or in fine, white, round river gravel. The latter is often preferred for paths and for the areas set aside for tables, benches, and recliners. For the garden of La Louve at Bonnieux, blue pebbles were chosen; their muted colors harmonize with the various stonework features—stone slabs, edging, benches, and troughs, interspersed with boxwood hedging and hollyhocks. The surrounds of the ornamental ponds and water features are usually paved with large stone slabs. Over time these have turned the same color as the statuary and the fountains, features that are so welcome in a land where the drought lasts for months at a time.

In his garden at La Londe (*above*), the nurseryman Jean-Marie Rey has chosen to cover the pergola with very thin canes that filter the light and air. A terrace paved with field-stone (*facing page*) is shaded by an almond tree that blossoms in February, a harbinger of spring.

WATER FEATURES

<T>his is an indispensable feature in our gardens, the symbol of refreshment and a sign of life in the sweltering heat of summer. It is hard to live here without being able to listen to the splash of water; it also offers refreshment for domestic animals, birds, and hedgehogs. The nurseryman Jean-Marie Rey, a specialist in Mediterranean plants, has installed large glazed water jars in his private garden, almost adjacent to the gravel terrace. They are planted with water lilies and are a novel way of introducing a water feature.

The value of a house, especially a *mas*, whose family and land demands heavy water consumption, has always been measured in terms of the abundance of well water, the presence of a spring, or the closeness of a river. "A huge and very handsome *mas* that has no water is a dead one," wrote Jean-Luc Massot. "A tumbledown *mas* that has a spring is worth more than a *bastide* in these parts." There is, of course, the famous story by Marcel Pagnol, in which the hardworking farmer Jean de Florette, whose spring has been deliberately blocked by neighbors, is driven to ruin and death.

Water was yet another external trapping of wealth for the châteaux and *bastides* inspired by Versailles, and the fountain-maker had an important job, at least until the waters of the Canal de Provence began to irrigate all the local farms and made it unnecessary to capture and store water. But in Provence, water is never wasted or lost. The water of the fountains and basins travel round in a closed circuit. The water comes from water-butts and tanks situated high up on the retaining walls, on the old water-tower principle. This provides the water

A garden in Provence cannot be pleasing without water; the splash and tinkle of fountains can be heard even in the smallest of gardens. An antique kitchen sink *(above)* has been given a new lease of life at Eygalières in the Alpilles, and a handsome fountain *(facing page)* with a gadrooned stone basin at Val Joanis in the Luberon.

162

pressure for the kitchen faucet before running down into the washtub and troughs, and it is then used to water the kitchen garden and the rest of the plants.

A reasonably large pond or pool surrounded by trees will provide shade and coolness through evaporation. It is easy to find a place for a fountain, even in the smallest garden. A waterspout in the shape of a mask and a basin can be acquired from sellers of recycled materials, and lends style to the plainest exterior. A fashion for statuary arrived alongside that for pools. In the seventeenth century, the Genoese became wealthy by growing olive trees and grapevines. They used their money to build *bastides* with elaborate gardens, copied from Italian Renaissance originals. The local inhabitants adapted these to their taste, making them one of the typical features of the region.

The swimming pool *(left)* at the Mas Dargent in Saint-Rémy is cool and refreshing, the modern equivalent of ponds and shady trees. A terra-cotta vase filled with water is planted with water lilies *(top left)*, while an antique kitchen sink and its ancient brass faucet temper the summer heat *(top right)*.

165

GARDEN FURNITURE

A classic garden is not complete without a stone bench
on which one can sun oneself in winter and sit in the
shade in summer. Gazebos *(above)*, and iron-and-wood
garden furniture *(facing page)* are easy to find at
antique dealers, or can be made by local craftsmen.
Gérard Aude is a blacksmith working in wrought iron,
and he is shown at work *(overleaf)* with some of his
creations. The plainest items, the chairs, have seats and
backs made of worked sheet iron.

If the sun is welcome from October to May, at other
times of the year it is vital to live in the shade.
Deciduous trees are particularly suitable for planting—
ideal for the purpose are plane trees, Spanish chestnuts,
false acacias or black locus trees, or a row of mulberry
trees or oaks, such as at La Mignarde, at Aix-en-
Provence. A clump of umbrella pines populated by
singing crickets, such as those that shade some of the
mas in the Camargue, is a real gift.

The natural shade is supplemented by the trellises
and pergolas attached to the façade, the most famous
being the muscat-grape trellis that gave its name to the
house in Saint-Tropez owned by the writer, Colette.
Pergolas and arbors also provide shade on the terrace
or in the garden. They are often roofed with canes that
filter light and air and throw a pattern of sun splashes
onto the paving stones. They are at their best when covered with wistaria, which flowers in early spring even
before the foliage appears, as long as it is on a south-
facing wall. Bougainvillea and jasmine flourish in
southern Provence and throughout the Nice district,
climbing riotously around wooden or bamboo poles, as
in the garden of Val Rahmeh, in Menton, where round
stone columns in the classical style, or square pillars
topped with a capital hold a wooden trellis in place; this
in turn is planted with real hanging gardens. Even the
humblest villa boasts decorative wrought-ironwork, trellises, and arbors. The owner of Le Club 55, a restaurant
at Pampelonne, created the framework of the bower that
covers the terrace using wooden flotsam and jetsam
thrown up on the beach after winter storms.

Mireille Desana makes unusual wooden furniture from flotsam and jetsam washed up on the beaches of the Rhône Delta *(facing page* and *below).* Two small garden chairs and a collection of tiny songbird cages *(left)* outside an old house in Fontaine de Vaucluse.

Beneath this shade, life carries on peacefully. One can lounge on deckchairs made from teak or wrought iron, on well-padded recliners—their pillows and mattresses an invitation to laziness, or sit in wicker chairs with round padded seats to make them more comfortable. Here and there, dotted around the terrace and in the garden, there are side tables and folding iron chairs with wooden seats, also well cushioned. These are for sitting while reading or chatting, far from the bustle of the household and its guests. All these chairs are an opportunity to display Provençal fabrics, which can be used to cushion or to cover disparate items of furniture in order to make them look like a set.

Tables that need to accommodate a large number of diners are generally rectangular, with a framework of painted wood or wrought iron and a table top of Salernes tiles or enamel.

Many antique dealers specialize in old wrought-iron furniture. It can also be found at antique fairs and street markets, especially on the Isle-sur-la-Sorgue, or it can be bought from local forges. Modern, simplified ironwork designs harmonize perfectly with the style of old farmhouses and country houses.

171

EARTHENWARE POTS

The supremacy of the *vase d'Anduze* is the result of pieces
such as this one *(above)*, with its lovely medallion of a child's
head. Pots, jars, and vases of terra-cotta prevail in the
garden because they allow the water to evaporate gradually
so that the plants do not overheat *(facing page)*. A range
of garden pots *(overleaf)* includes various classic designs
from La Poterie Provençale at Biot, Ravel pots from
Aubagne, and the red-and-green enameled *vase d'Anduze*,
whose coat of arms proclaims its origin.

Bright colors prevail in Provence. They can be found
in the stucco, fabrics, walls and, of course, the
garden. Terra-cotta paving and pots contribute a
reddish-pink, faded rose, and there are the bright green
and ocher of the glazes with an infinity of shapes:
flowerpots, pot-bellied urns, and vases on steady, round
bases; stone and earthenware jars of every provenance,
once used for storing preserves and perishable foods
and now used for growing plants. This profusion of containers is designed solely to satisfy the Provençal love
of flowers, revealed in the bright patches of color on the
terraces, retaining walls, and gardens.

Although classic terra-cotta flowerpots are made
throughout the region, varying only in the color of the
local clay, large garden pots such as jars, urns, vases, and
planters come from well-known potteries.

The oldest known jars come from Biot. Some are
glazed inside and were used to hold oil, wine, or brine;
others are of plain, unglazed terra-cotta. Jars are still made
in Biot, at the Poterie Provençale for instance. They may
be wide, oval, or pot-bellied, and they stand in terrace
corners, or beside garden paths overflowing with pelargo-
niums and petunias. They may be antique, or merely old,
and they have a patina that makes them look as if they
have stood in the garden since time immemorial.

The clay deposits of Saint-Zacharie, close to Aubagne,
produce a yellowish clay which has been used for more
than a century to make large pots decorated with garlands, and fluted jars that can be bought from Ravel.
Their softness to the touch makes them instantly
recognizable. Large, rustic pots, in the classic, almost

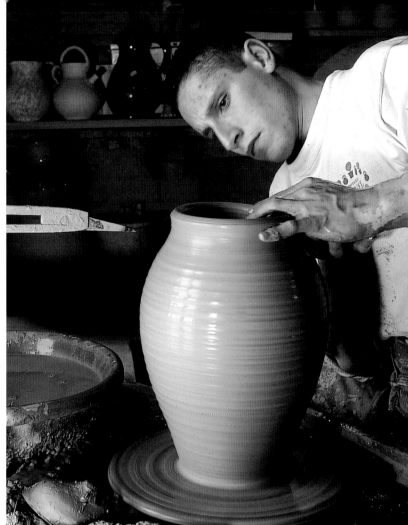

cylindrical shape, with a wide base, are often planted with shaped boxwood or pittosporum.

The big pots known as *vases d'Anduze* are used to hold all types of plants, but especially orange trees. These are the type of pots that were used at Versailles, though there they were much more elaborate. They are made almost exclusive by two potteries, Les Enfants de Boisset in Anduze, and La Poterie La Madeleine at Tornac. The shape is inspired by the Medici vases, and the decoration—flower or fruit garlands—runs around the famous coat of arms that is the mark of their authenticity. When they are genuine antiques, the peeling glaze reveals a pale layer of slip covering the terra-cotta, on top of which the green, yellow, or brown jasper is laid before the final transparent glaze known as alquifoux is applied

by the potters of Dieulefit. These pots are one of the most typical ornaments of the gardens of Provence.

If Biot jars and Ravel pots, which are almost velvety to the touch, line the retaining walls or stand beside the low hedges of the garden paths, the *vases d'Anduze* are just as attractive in the sunshine, standing alone in a corner of the terrace, under leaf fronds, where the light plays on the bright glaze as it filters through the foliage, as at the Clos Peyronnet, one of the loveliest gardens in Menton. They make a treasured gift for weddings or any other celebration, because the material and colors represent the quintessence of Provençal country crafts.

Antique jars are used to support this table *(above)*, the creative idea of an antique dealer at Isle-sur-la-Sorgue.

All the craftspeople who have been mentioned in the text, or whose work has been photographed for the book, are listed here, classified according to the chapters in which they appear, as well as by the département in France in which they and their workshops or stores are located. In addition to these there are also addresses giving stockists of building materials, furniture, decorative or everyday objects, tableware, and pottery. The addresses of stockists in France are given under the relevant chapter, and a list of suppliers of Provençal goods outside France is given on page 187. Such lists cannot be exhaustive, of course, and we would be pleased to hear other suggestions from our readers. The addresses have been collected in order to help anyone who wants to remodel, redecorate, or even build a Provençal house, and is designed to enable readers to become their own decorator. Consequently, we have not provided the names of those architects and interior designers who have created magnificent homes in Provence. On the other hand, we have added a list of the most picturesque guesthouses, because staying in them is the best way to discover and appreciate the delights of a beautiful house in Provence.

I. A HOME IN THE SUN

FÉDÉRATION NATIONALE DES CAUE
(Architectural, development control, and environmental services)
—Bouches-du-Rhône representative
35, Rue Montgrand
13006 **Marseilles**
Tel: 04 91 33 02 02
—Var representative
All. J. Moulin
83150 **Bandol**
Tel: 04 94 29 37 45
—Vaucluse representative
4, Rue Petite-Calade
84000 **Avignon**
Tel: 04 90 85 29 35
Specialists in architectural style, and local planning and zoning rules. A valuable source of information when remodeling or renovating.

RECYCLED MATERIALS

Les Matériaux d'Antan
RN7 Route d'Avignon
13540 **Puyricard**
Tel: 04 42 92 62 12
Stone-cutter.

André Combet
Le Village
26300 **Charpey**
Tel : 04 75 59 80 49
Recycled roof tiles, roof-beams, and fireplaces.

RCB Carrelages
Quartier de la Chaux
83360 **Grimaud**
Tel: 04 98 12 60 10
House-building materials and terra-cotta.

Décor et Tradition
Les Hauts Banquets
84300 **Cavaillon**
Tel: 04 90 06 05 77
Purchase and sale of antique materials; fountains, sculptures, fireplaces, doors, etc.

Provence Vieux Matériaux
Le Camp
84300 **Cavaillon**
Tel: 04 90 78 28 12
Fireplaces, paving slabs, decorative stonework.

Jean Chabaud
ZI route de Gargas
84400 **Apt**
Tel: 04 90 74 07 61

Antique materials, ceramic tiles, fireplaces, and other decorative items.

Alessio Pierre et Fils
Rue de la Mairie
84750 **Viens**
Tel: 04 90 75 33 38
Dealers in old stone slabs for dressing façades or paving.

Provence Retrouvée
Route d'Apt
84800 **L'Isle-sur-la-Sorgue**
Tel: 04 90 38 52 62
Recycled materials and stone flooring slabs.

QUARRY STONE AND TILES

La Pierre et le Marbre
870, Avenue des Paluds
13400 **Aubagne**
For façades, Cassis stone flooring, Pont-du-Gard stone, etc.

Atelier Didier Tocco
ZA des Arnajons
13610 **Le Puy-Ste-Réparade**
Tel: 04 42 61 84 33
Stone basins, fountains, fireplaces.

Pierres Blanches de Provence
4, Avenue des Baux
13990 **Fontvieille**
Tel: 04 90 54 64 65
Stone-carving, fountains, stone flooring, urns.

Dutto Frères
Rue Saint-Jean
83170 **Brignoles**
Stonework, stone lintels for doors and windows, stone staircases, roof tiles, stone basins, columns, porches, paving slabs, etc.

Les Matériaux du Littoral
Chemin du Peyrat
ZI de Grimaud
83310 **Grimaud**
Tel: 04 94 43 26 64
Stone-cutting; also sells balustrades, fountains, troughs, ponds, garden ornaments, etc.

Carrières la Menerbienne
SA Serres Frères et Cie
84560 **Menerbes**
Tel: 04 90 72 23 60
External and interior paving slabs, balustrades, stone-facing and cladding.

DOORS AND SHUTTERS

Antique doors
Route d'Avignon
13210 **St-Rémy-de-Provence**
Tel: 04 90 92 13 13
Refurbishment of old doors,
cabinet-making, patination,
wrought-iron work.

Les Belles Portes de Provence
Route de la Valliguières
30126 **Tavel**
Tel: 04 66 50 03 42
Specialist maker of doors in
patinated wood; traditional
or antiqued patinas.

Les Mille et Une Portes
4 and 9, Place Émile-Zola
83570 **Carcès**
Tel: 04 94 04 50 27
Antique dealer specializing
in doors and paneling.

Boiseries et Décorations
Quartier Castagne
Route de Murs
84400 **Gargas**
Tel: 04 90 74 15 71
Restoration of doors and old
porticos and stoops. Thousands of antique doors on
display. The company also
makes doors, window-
frames, and shutters.

ROOFING

Les Roseaux de Camargue
12, route de Saint-Gilles
30600 **Vauvert**
Tel: 04 66 88 22 84
Reeds are sold in bundles by
Monsieur Prevost, who can
construct a traditional
thatched roof or restore
a thatched cottage.

**Association des Sagneurs
de Petite Camargue**
Tel: 04 66 87 21 07
This is the association of
thatchers; they work
with *saigne*, the reed that
grows and is harvested in
the Camargue, between
the Petit Rhône and
Aigues-Mortes.

Claude Delton
Grand Péreyrole
84110 **Vaison-la-Romaine**
Tel: 04 90 28 98 01
Weathervanes for decorating
roofs. An inspired designer.

PAINTS

Olivier Delaye
L'Olivaie
147, Chemin de Saint-Jean
06130 **Grasse**
Tel: 04 93 09 21 15
Working from a 17th-century
sheepfold in Grasse, this
painter creates high-quality
interiors and exteriors.

A & D Façades
Quartier Saint-Marc
83170 **Camps-la-Source**
Tel: 04 94 80 84 84
Specialist in renovating
façades made of every
material; colored wash and
plaster in traditional colors.

II. INTERIORS

OCHER AND TEXTURING

Stuc et Matières
1486, Chemin de la Plaine
06250 **Mougins**
Tel: 04 92 28 57 98
Typically Mediterranean
texturing and acrylic waxes.

La Stafferie
Chemin du Defoussat
06480 **La Colle-sur-Loup**
Tel: 04 93 32 88 64
Craft plasterwork for the
most elegant interiors, lime
wash, traditional polishes.

Ariel Balmassière
Hôtel Fransure de Fabri
2, Rue Port-Royal
30700 **Uzès**
Tel: 04 66 22 16 03

From colored frontages in
ocher or pink lime wash, to
cornices, gables, ironwork,
and shutters, the whole
Provençal palette is here.

Gianni Prouvost
BP 4019
83069 **Toulon Cedex**
Tel: 04 94 91 44 80
President of the "Couleurs et
Traditions de Provence"
Association, his office
advises on all types of paint
and coatings, including lime
washes as well as ocher-
based paints.

Les Trois Matons
337, Route de la Farlède
83130 **La Garde**
Tel: 04 94 14 93 95
This firm restored the house
frontages at Hyères. As color
scheme experts for interior
and exterior walls, they work
on very few sites themselves,
but train others and provide
referrals. They also sell terra-
cotta, pigments, oxides, and
ready-mixed products.

La Maison de Juliette
353, Avenue de la Résistance
83190 **Ollioules**
Tel: 04 94 63 73 08
Firm specializing in pierced
woodwork and friezes to
decorate doors and alcoves.
This type of intricate wood-
carving used to decorate flyscreens in the past.

**Conservatoire des Ocres
et Pigments Appliqués**
former Usine Mathieu
Association OKHRA
Route d'Apt D-104
84200 **Roussillon**
Tel: 04 90 05 66 69
Long-established ocher
factory in which amateurs
and professionals can learn
different techniques using
water-based paints and
lime washes.

Établissement Chauvin
Avenue de Viton
84400 **Apt**
Tel: 04 90 74 21 68
The place to buy natural
ocher, oxides, and colors for
tinting lime wash for house
frontages.

Oxyde 84
248, Ave. Philippe-de-Girard
84400 **Apt**
Tel: 06 62 26 74 78
This is the showroom of
Noémie Verguas, a specialist
in interior paintwork and
lime washes.

**Société des Ocres de
France**
Impasse des Ocriers
84400 **Apt**
Tel: 04 90 74 63 82
Monsieur and Madame
Guigou are the last ocher producers in Europe. They own a
quarry in Gargas from which
they extract the yellow earth
used to make paints and
lime washes.

Vincent Tripard
298, Voie Domitienne
84400 **Apt**
Tel: 04 90 74 64 48
A master craftsman; a specialist in coatings and traditional lime washes for walls.

Patrice Arnoud
Mas Piédache
84580 **Oppède**
Tel: 04 90 76 99 08
Interior decorator.

Comme en Été
6, Place Ferdinand-Buisson
84800 **L'Isle-sur-la-Sorgue**
Tel: 04 90 21 10 46
Store created by Anne
Saurin, an interior architect.

Les Plafonds de l'Isle
ZA Petite Marine
84800 **L'Isle-sur-la-Sorgue**
Tel: 04 90 38 14 47

Makes old-fashioned Provençal coffered wood-and-plaster ceilings.

MANTELPIECES AND FIREPLACES

Jean Zunino
635, Chemin de Jalassières
13510 **Éguilles**
Tel: 04 42 64 12 38
Old-fashioned stone and wood mantelpieces.

Alain Gauthey
Route de Draguignan
83630 **Salernes**
Tel: 04 94 70 60 77
Restores and copies old stone mantelpieces.

FLOORING

L'Atelier de la Terre Cuite
2610, route d'Avignon
La Calade
13090 **Aix-en-Provence**
Tel: 04 42 96 18 65
Maker of white clay handmade tiles, copied from old models, fired in a wood-fired kiln. For walls, he produces red oxide, red ocher, lavender blue, and other paints.

Carocim
1515, Rte du Puy Ste Réparade
13089 **Aix-en-Provence**
Tel: 04 42 92 20 39
Batch-dyed cement tiles for floors and walls; tiling and friezes laid in brightly colored patterns, including designs by key contemporary designers. Carocim has also produced exclusive tiling for Souleiado.
Photos pp. 70 and 75

Terres Cuites des Launes
Quartier des Launes
83630 **Salernes**
Tel: 04 94 70 62 72
Tomettes and tiles made in the traditional way (fired in a wood-fired kiln).
Photo p. 73

Atelier Pierre Basset
Quartier des Arnauds
83630 **Salernes**
Tel: 04 94 70 70 70
Terra-cotta tiles. An impressive collection of hundreds of handmade, decorated tiles, and colored square tiles with an antique patina.

Carrelages Pierre Boutal
Route de Draguignan
83630 **Salernes**
Tel: 04 94 70 62 12
Hand-painted tiles and plain red and yellow tiles for old-fashioned kitchens.

Atelier Alain Vagh
Route d'Entrecasteaux
83630 **Salernes**
Tel: 04 94 70 61 85
Here traditional tiling makes way for original modern creations by Alain Vagh.

Atelier Sismondini
Route de Sillans
83630 **Salernes**
Tel: 04 94 04 63 06
Authentic, plain, and natural terra-cotta flooring, made in the traditional way and baked in a wood-fired kiln.

Carrelages Polidori
Route de Draguignan
83690 **Salernes**
Tel: 04 94 70 61 86
Terra-cotta, glazed tiles, and enameled surfaces for garden tables and kitchens.

Les Émaux de Provence
Route de Draguignan
83690 **Salernes**
Tel: 04 94 67 58 79
An excellent resource: traditional savoir-faire combined with modern designs.

Carrelages Maurin
Route de Draguignan
83690 **Salernes**
Tel: 04 94 70 64 78
The tiny workshop is used to produce tiles, hand-printed in the traditional way.

Jacques Brest
Quartier des Arnauds
83690 **Salernes**
Tel: 04 94 70 60 65
Tomettes, trefoil tiles, Moorish tiles, molded and cut by hand in the traditional way.
Photos p. 73

**Association
Terres de Salernes**
Tel: 04 94 67 47 41
Information about craftspeople.

Porodécor
43, Rue Ampère
83000 **Toulon**
Tel: 04 94 21 90 88
A master craftsman specializing in tiled flooring. Useful for polishing or aging terra-cotta tiling; or conversely for brightening its pastel colors.

Vernin
RN 100 Pont-Julien
84480 **Bonnieux**
Tel: 04 90 04 63 04
Handmade and hand-glazed tiles in 165 colors. Tiles may be pale, pink, or red terra-cotta; glazed, hexagonal, or in the Aix trefoil pattern.
Photos pp. 72–75

Les Tapis d'Entrecasteaux
Rue Émile-Miramont
83570 **Entrecasteaux**
Tel: 04 94 04 44 90
Hand-woven jute or sisal rugs (imported fiber), made to order. Can be colored and reversible. To throw over tiles to make the floor warmer.

**Manufacture
des Tapis de Cogolin**
Boulevard Louis-Blanc
83310 **Cogolin**
Tel: 04 94 55 70 65
Wool or cotton rugs hand-woven on ancient looms, created to order.

BEAD CURTAINS

M. et Mme Dieudonné
339, rue des Vieux-Remparts
84100 **Orange**
Tel: 04 90 34 82 47
Bead curtains in boxwood, wood, plastic, etc.

Marie-Claude Brochet
1043, Avenue des Vertes-Rives
84140 **Montfavet**
Tel: 04 90 23 58 37
Handmade boxwood bead curtains.

MUSEUMS AND CHÂTEAUX

Many houses in Provence are open to the public, displaying furniture, faïence, and fabrics. Some châteaux are also open.

Musée Masséna
65, Rue de France
06000 **Nice**
Tel: 04 93 88 11 34
Provençal and Niçe furniture, faïence from Marseilles, Apt, and Moustiers.

**Musée d'Art et d'Histoire
de Provence**
2, Rue Mirabeau
06130 **Grasse**
Tel: 04 93 36 01 61
Furniture and items from the daily life of former times, housed in the old Clapiers-Cabris mansion.

Museon Arlaten
29, Rue de la République
13200 **Arles**
Tel: 04 90 96 08 23
This attractive museum displays all the furniture and implements used on a *mas*.

Musée du Vieil Aix
17, Rue Gaston-de-Saporta
13100 **Aix-en-Provence**
Tel: 04 42 21 43 55
Furniture, pottery, etc., all housed in a magnificent 17th-century mansion.

Hôtel d'Olivary
Rue du 4-Septembre
13100 **Aix-en-Provence**
Tel: 04 42 26 86 01
This 17th-century mansion
includes a row of three
adjoining reception rooms
beautifully decorated with
overmantels and plaster-
work. The formal garden,
with its many trees, consti-
tutes an additional attrac-
tion. Visits must be arranged
by telephone beforehand.
Photos pp. 63, 68, 69, and 74

**Musée des Arts
et Traditions Populaires
du Terroir Marseillais
Château Gombert**
5, Place des Héros
13013 **Marseilles**
Tel: 04 91 68 14 38
Antique furniture, cookery
utensils, pottery.

Musée Grobet-Labadié
140, Boulevard Longchamp
13001 **Marseilles**
Tel: 04 91 62 21 82
A mansion that has retained
its original decor, the setting
for a lovely collection of furniture and faïence.

Château de Barbentane
1, Rue du Château
13570 **Barbentane**
Tel: 04 90 95 51 07
Lovely Provençal furniture
and a garden that is a delight
to discover.
*Photos pp. 18, 52, 53, 89, 94,
96, 134, and 135*

**Musée Provençal des Arts
et Traditions Populaires**
Place du Champ-de-Mars
26290 **Donzère**
Tel: 04 75 51 56 56

**Musée des Arts
et Traditions Populaires**
15, Rue Roumanille
83300 **Draguignan**
Tel: 04 94 47 05 72

Daily life in Provence;
features a lovely old kitchen.

Château d'Ansouis
84240 **Ansouis**
Tel: 04 90 09 82 70
This château is an excellent
example of the charm of the
stately homes of Provence.
*Photos pp. 20, 50, 59, 84, 86,
87, 95, 108, 109, and 154*

Château de Lourmarin
84160 **Lourmarin**
Tel: 04 90 68 15 23
The loveliest floors and
ceilings in Provence, and
wonderful furniture, too.
*Photos pp. 57, 62, 66, 76, 77,
88, and 95*

III. FURNITURE AND FRAMES

ANTIQUE DEALERS AND
PRODUCERS OF COPIES
OF ANTIQUE FURNITURE;
CABINET-MAKERS

Antiquités Les Paillerols
Rue de la Bourgade
04360 **Moustiers-Sainte-
Marie**
Tel: 04 92 74 60 07
Provençal antiques.

Henri de Tonge
93, Rue Antibes
06400 **Cannes**
Tel: 04 93 39 20 00
Traditional furniture,
kitchens made to order,
painted chairs, etc.

Jean-François Roehrig
15, Rue Saint-Esprit
06600 **Antibes Juan-les-Pins**
Tel: 04 93 34 54 84
Cabinet-maker, finest quality
restoration work.

La Chaise de Provence
1, Rue Saint-Pierre
13005 **Marseilles**
Tel: 04 91 47 98 96
Nearly a hundred examples

of traditional seating, re-
rushing and re-caning of
chairs mechanically or
by hand.

Patines Anciennes
169, Rue Paradis
13006 **Marseilles**
Tel: 04 91 37 21 91
Furniture manufacturer,
copies of antique models.

Jean-Luc Kieffer
237, Promenade de la
Corniche-Kennedy
13007 **Marseilles**
Tel: 04 91 31 71 25
Restoration of chests of
drawers, cabinets, chairs.

Félix-Ailhaud
1, rue du Quatre-Septembre
13100 **Aix-en-Provence**
Tel: 04 42 27 96 69
Francis Guaré, an antique
dealer, operates under this
name. He restores and recre-
ates old furniture, such as
chests, bergères, and corner
cabinets in patinated wood.
Photos pp. 94, 95, and 99

Meubles Babsky
Route de Saint-Rémy
13103 **Mas-Blanc-des-
Alpilles**
Tel: 04 90 49 08 18/60
Restores and copies painted
solid wood furniture.

Galerie L'été
ZAC du Roubian
13150 **Tarascon**
Tel: 04 90 91 36 13
Creates and personalizes
finishes for the charming
"Provençal Collection."
Another collection, "Classic,"
is for hotels and restaurants.
Catalog available by post.

Faïsse et Plata
Rue Copernic
13200 **Arles**
Tel: 04 90 96 71 25
Workshop and showroom for

lovely Provençal furniture,
including chests, closets, and
sideboards.

Frédéric Dervieux
5, Rue Vernon
13200 **Arles**
Tel: 04 90 96 02 39
A store inside a very lovely
mansion. Specializes in
Provençal furniture.

Gilles Roland
Z.I. Nord
14, Rue Jacques-Lieutaud
13200 **Arles**
Wrought-iron stair-rails and
balustrading.

Coup de Soleil
10, Avenue Frédéric-Mistral
13210 **Saint-Rémy-de-Provence**
Tel: 04 32 60 09 85
Chairs and painted furniture.

Mireille Desana
Route Départementale 570
13460 **Saintes-Maries
de-la-Mer**
Tel: 04 90 97 72 15
Baroque furniture created
from driftwood for interiors
and gardens.

Antiquités du Braban
Route de Bellecroix
13520 **Le Paradou**
A wonderful choice of
antiques displayed in a
superb *bastide*.

Bernard Paul
Rue de République
13810 **Eygalières**
Tel: 04 90 95 97 86
Antique furniture and
objects.

René Lacroix
30300 **Vallabrègues**
Tel: 04 66 59 20 59
Provençal chairs with
crossed stretchers, as well
as *radassiés* made in the
traditional style.

Ets Monleau
30300 **Vallabrègues**
Tel: 04 66 59 20 17
Provençal chairs and *radassiés* painted with old patterns (Arlesian and wheat ears, for example).

Bruno Carles
209–235 Ave. du Maréchal-de-Lattre-de-Tassigny
34400 **Lunel**
Tel: 04 67 71 36 10
For everything that once decorated the *bastide*, such as orange tree pots (*vases d'Anduze*), superb chairs, rush-bottomed *radassiés*, painted furniture, and bookcases.

Lou Pichot Trésor
4, Rue Jean Aicard
83230 **Bormes-les-Mimosas**
Tel: 04 94 71 26 23
Antiques and rare objects in a lovely house.

Les Meubles du Luc
N97 Route de Toulon
83340 **Le Luc**
Tel: 04 94 60 70 76
Traditional walnut, oak, and cherrywood solid wood furniture. Painted or restored furniture and chairs.

Atelier Garance
4, Rue du 11-Novembre
83470 **Pourrières**
Tel: 04 94 78 50 43
Isabelle Barale specializes in furniture restoration. She brings life back to old polished, painted, or varnished furniture stored in lofts, and applies a patina that is appropriate to the decor of the room.

Gérard Bertolotto
5, Rue Camille-Desmoulins
83610 **Collobrières**
Tel: 04 94 48 00 79
Painted furniture in pure Provençal tradition, in pale yellow and olive green.

Jacqueline Soulard
Château de Deffends
83780 **Flayosquet**
Tel: 04 94 70 40 37
Buys and sells antique Provençal furniture.

Ferdinand Dervieux
11, Rue Félix-Gras
84000 **Avignon**
Tel: 04 90 82 14 37
Provençal furniture and antiques.

Bernard Paul
19 *ter*, Rue de la Petite-Fusterie
84000 **Avignon**
Tel: 04 90 86 80 94
Provençal antiques and objects.

Gérard Guerre
1, Plan du Lunel
84000 **Avignon**
Tel: 04 90 86 42 67
Installed in the beautiful mansion of Laurens, Gérard Guerre is an antique dealer who deals in Provençal furniture and other items. He is the author of *Les Arts décoratifs en Provence du XVIIIe au XIXe siècle*.

Vox Populi
54, Rue Joseph-Vernet
84000 **Avignon**
Tel: 04 90 85 70 25
Pascale Palun uses ancient and recycled materials to create very original decorations.

Jean-Pierre Magnan
8 *bis*, Rue Mazeau
84100 **Orange**
Tel: 04 90 34 25 62
Craft workshop making furniture including a Provençal range of closets and chests in polished wood. No chairs.

Ateliers Laffanour
91, Avenue de la Libération
84150 **Jonquières**
Tel: 04 90 70 60 82

Provençal furniture made in the traditional way, *radassiés*, chairs, painted, polished, or patinated to look like antiques.

Guy Chaboissier
238, Avenue Notre-Dame-de-Santé
84200 **Carpentras**
Tel: 04 90 67 04 18
Re-rushing of Provençal chairs.

Catherine Pergay
283, Avenue Notre-Dame-de-Santé
84200 **Carpentras**
Tel: 04 90 63 18 59
She creates painted furniture using the full range of Provençal colors.

J.-M. Roux
22, Boulevard Louis-Giraud
84200 **Carpentras**
Tel: 04 90 63 06 81
Restoration of antique furniture.

Albert Doursin
Quartier Fontblanque,
712 Chemin Gente
84210 **Pernes-les-Fontaines**
Tel: 04 90 61 65 39
Traditional Provençal furniture of very good quality.

Brocante 11
11, Avenue des Quatre-Otages
84800 **L'Isle-sur-la-Sorgue**
Tel: 04 90 38 21 02
In this tiny store, Philippe and Marlise de Font-Réaulx have accumulated a number of delightful curiosities.

Le Mas de Curebourg
Hélène Dampeine
Route d'Apt
84800 **L'Isle-sur-la-Sorgue**
Tel: 04 90 20 30 06
Provençal furniture, *radassiés*, lovely antiques, and copies of traditional pieces.

Antiquités Yves Boussin
7, Avenue des Quatre-Otages
84800 **L'Isle-sur-la-Sorgue**
Tel: 04 90 20 69 93

Objets de Hasard, Antiquités
13, Avenue des Quatre-Otages
84800 **L'Isle-sur-la-Sorgue**
Tel: 04 90 38 54 58

Antiquités Danièle Capia-Taillant
7, Avenue des Quatre-Otages
84800 **L'Isle-sur-la-Sorgue**
Tel: 04 90 20 69 93
Provençal furniture, glazed pottery, and reproductions of rush-bottomed chairs.

Bertrand Colombier et Bruno Dion, Antiquités
7, Avenue des Quatre-Otages
84800 **L'Isle-sur-la-Sorgue**
Tel: 04 90 38 62 95
For the orange color and brilliance of the ceramics.

Village des Antiquaires
M. and Mme Nicod
84800 **L'Isle-sur-la-Sorgue**
Tel: 04 90 38 04 57 / 20 38
Old pine furniture and decorative objects.

Antiquités Nathalie Légier
Avenue des Quatre-Otages
84800 **L'Isle-sur-la-Sorgue**
Tel: 06 90 20 75 17
Provençal furniture and 18th- and 19th-century solid wood items, chairs, *radassiés*, pottery.

Mémoires d'un Âne
Jean-Jacques Bourgeois
5, Avenue des 4-Otages
84800 **L'Isle-sur-la-Sorgue**
Tel: 04 90 20 63 15
Antiques, decoration, chairs, and small 18th-century Provencal furnishings, pottery, and tableware. Jean-Jacques Bourgeois is the author of *L'Âge d'or du*

siège paillé, Éd. Massin.
*Photos pp. 55, 100, 119, 126,
141, and 171*

Le Mas de Flore
Pierre Degrugillier
84800 **Lagnes**
Tel: 04 90 20 37 96
Antiques and very original
furniture are sold from this
old *mas*.
Photo p. 97

Sifas
Stores in Aix-en-Provence,
Saint-Tropez, Fréjus, Cannes,
Antibes, Nice, Paris. List of
outlets at:
04 42 18 60 80
Their "Luberon" line of furniture is in patinated wood
(in 24 colors); they also make
curving, patinated wrought
iron for bedrooms.

État de Siège
21, Avenue de Friedland
75008 **Paris**
Tel: 01 42 56 64 75
This Parisian shop sells
Provençal furniture made in
Provence to classic designs,
including *radassiés* and
chairs.

IV. CERAMICS AND GLASSWARE

Jean-Nicolas Gérard
4, Rue du Fbg-Ratonneau
04210 **Valensole**
Tel: 04 92 74 98 41
Glazed earthenware, tableware, yellow, green, and
blue plates.

Atelier Bondil
Place de l'Église
04360 **Moustiers-Ste-
Marie**
Tel: 04 92 74 67 02
Louis XV-style china deco-
rated with foliage and birds
in blue, ocher, and green.
Painting demonstrations are
staged at the store.

L'Atelier de Ségriès
Route de Riez
04360 **Moustiers-Ste-
Marie**
Tel: 04 92 74 66 69
Hand-painted pottery, using
antique designs and motifs.
Dinner services, pitchers,
vases, candlesticks.

Atelier Soleil
Chemin de Quinson
04360 **Moustiers-Ste-
Marie**
Tel: 04 92 74 63 05
Frank Scherer designs,
makes, and decorates pot-
tery in the tradition of the
manufactories of Moustiers.
White dishes with Berain
decoration and more
modern bowls.

Foucard-Jourdan
65 *bis*, rue Georges-Clemenceau
06220 **Vallauris**
Tel: 04 93 64 66 38
The main source of table-
ware, authentic Provençal
art pottery.

Galerie Madoura
Rue Suzanne-et-Georges-
Ramié
06220 **Vallauris**
Tel: 04 93 64 66 39

Lou Pignatier
G. Compas
43, rue Georges-Clemenceau
06220 **Vallauris**
Tel: 04 93 64 85 95
Handmade pottery table-
ware, lead-free, glazed earthenware in Provençal colors.

Bernard Soleil
Route du Col-Saint-Roch
06390 **Coaraze**
Tel: 04 93 79 31 78
Studio potter.

Jacqueline Morabito
42–44, Rue Yves-Klein
06480 **La-Colle-sur-Loup**
Tel: 04 93 32 64 91

This decorator has created a
line of white earthenware for
elegant tables. *Photo p. 126*

**Les Faïenceries
Mentonnaises**
14 *bis*, Promenade
du Val-de-Menton
06500 **Menton**
Handmade faïence
decorated with lemons
and leaves.

Frank Boselli
437, Chemin Brague
06740 **Châteauneuf-de-Grasse**
Tel: 04 93 60 11 81
This craftsman makes olive-
wood salad bowls, and other
items in the local tradition.

Santons Arterra
1a, Rue du Petit-Puits
13002 **Marseilles**
Tel: 04 91 91 03 31
Of all the makers of *santons*, it
is this one who has made the
particularly decorative farandole dancer.
Photos pp. 4, and 6–7

Faïencerie Figueres et Fils
10–12, Avenue Lauzier
13008 **Marseilles**
Tel: 04 91 73 06 79
Compositions of fruits and
vegetables in ceramic
trompe-l'œil.

Claude Massucco
Quartier Camp Major,
Villa Claude
13400 **Aubagne**
Tel: 04 42 03 34 31
The last potter in Aubagne to
follow the local tradition of
making *tarraïettes*, earthenware miniatures.

Poterie Ravel
Avenue des Goums
13400 **Aubagne**
Tel: 04 42 82 42 00
Traditional tableware, dinner
services, and garden urns .
Photos pp. 174 and 175

Poterie des Quatre Chemins
Les Quatre Chemins
de Saint-Jean
13400 **Aubagne**
Tel: 04 42 32 07 27
White ceramic with pale
blue decoration. Pitchers,
dishes, teapots, etc.

**Maison Louis Sicard-Amy
Atelier d'Art Sylvette Amy**
2, Boulevard Émile-Combes
13400 **Aubagne**
Tel: 04 42 70 12 92
The famous manufacturer of
pottery crickets still makes
his traditional yellow and
red-patterned china, originally created in the 1930s
and still very popular.

Le Lys Amelié
Chemin du Pont-Mont-Blanc
13520 **Maussane**
Tel: 04 90 54 37 55
Lovely craft pottery and
vases d'Anduze in the
Provençal tradition.

Poterie de Haute Provence
Route de Nyons
26220 **Dieulefit**
Tel: 04 75 46 42 10

Atelier du Sage
1, Place Chateauras
26220 **Dieulefit**
Tel: 04 75 46 35 25
Glazed yellow, green,
and blue tableware.
Designs based on Louis XV
silverware.

La Poterie Sourdive
26270 **Cliousclat**
Tel: 04 75 63 09 69
Flowerpots and tableware in
unusual shades of green and
yellow. A small museum on
the history of pottery is at
the bottom of the garden.

La Poterie d'Aigues-Vives
6 *bis*, Rue Victor-Hugo
30220 **Aigues-Mortes**
Tel: 04 66 53 81 62

Utilitarian pottery fired in an ancient wood-fired kiln. Dishes, pitchers, etc., are sold here and made nearby at Aigues-Vives.

Les Céramiques de Lussan
Route de St-Ambroix
30580 **Lussan**
Tel: 04 66 72 90 92
A very inspired potter, who creates decorative objects for the home.

Poterie Esteban
30670 **Aigues-Vives**
Tel: 04 66 35 18 79
Glazed earthenware mortars, dishes, and pitchers.

La Maison d'Uzès
18, Rue Docteur-Blanchard
30700 **Uzès**
Tel: 04 66 03 32 01
Martine de Fontanes receives visitors in an 18th-century mansion. Here she displays collections of antique china as well as modern china in bright colors. Pottery is also displayed in the garden, where lunch is served.
Photos pp. 106, 107, 110, 123–125, 128, 172, and 175

Véronique Pichon
19 *bis*, Avenue de la Gare
30700 **Uzès**
Tel: 04 66 22 19 53
Utilitarian and decorative glazed pottery.
Photo p. 116

Poterie des Trois-Terres
83316 **Grimaud**
Tel: 04 94 43 21 62
Workshop and showroom for pottery, red and bright yellow tableware, hand-painted tiles, brown and yellow miniature tiles.

Faïencerie de la Belle Époque
2, Rue de la Paix
83670 **Varages**
Tel: 04 94 77 64 95

M. Offner produces white faïence or patterned faïence on a white background for table and decoration.

Manufacture des Lauriers
Avenue de la Foux
83670 **Varages**
Tel: 04 94 77 64 79
Major manufacturer of utilitarian faïence, who makes ware for several brands (including Geneviève Lethu); it can be bought from the factory shop (address below).

Poterie du Château
Route de Draguignan
83690 **Salernes**
Tel: 04 94 70 63 40
Tians, basins in glazed earthenware, hand-turned pottery, roof tiles, flat or rounded tiles in glazed terra-cotta.
Photos pp. 73, 122, 123, and 129

Le Tian Provençal
Parking du Stade
83690 **Salernes**
Tel: 04 94 70 77 17
Tians and basins have made this potter's name, but he also makes balustrading to decorate terraces.

Poterie du Soleil
Le Colombier
83690 **Villecroze**
Tel: 04 94 67 52 42
Dinner services, useful and decorative objects made from red clay or stoneware. Very pure shapes.

Poterie Salernoise
Route de Draguignan
83690 **Salernes**
Tel: 04 94 70 64 82
This is the only Salernes pottery that makes tableware. The dinner services in green or yellow glazed earthenware, decorated with spirals, contribute a very modern note to summer tables.

Matteo
Rue Jean-Jacques-Rousseau
83690 **Salernes**
Tel: 04 94 70 74 94
Original painted china.

Terre è Provence
26, Rue de la République
84000 **Avignon**
Tel. (store): 04 90 85 56 45 /
04 90 16 52 52
Simple Dieulefit china in bright colors.

Côté Bastide
3, Rue du Grand-Pré
84160 **Lourmarin**
Tel: 04 90 08 57 92
In this delightful and well-hidden location, Nicole Houques sells ceramics and china, glasses and pitchers.

La Poterie de Pierroux
84220 **Roussillon**
Tel: 04 90 05 68 81
Pottery lessons.

Antony Pitot
Ponty, RN 100
84220 **Goult**
Tel: 04 90 72 22 79
Fine yellow or green faïence in the Apt tradition. This well-known potter accepts special commissions.

**Martine Gilles
and Jaap Wieman**
84390 **Brantes**
Tel: 04 75 28 03 37
This lovely hilltop village, north of Mont Ventoux, is also worth visiting for the ceramics workshop.
Photo p. 111

Yvon Feraille
Le Quai de la Gare,
Avenue Julien-Guigue
84800 **L'Isle-sur-la-Sorgue**
Lovely collection of faïences amassed by an expert.

For a list of dates of all the pottery fairs in France, write

to: **Marchés de Potiers**
Les Rues Godel
61370 **Echauffour**
fax: 02 33 34 50 52

SPECIALIST MUSEUMS

Le Musée de la Faïence
Place du Presbytère
04360 **Moustiers-Sainte-Marie**
Tel: 04 92 74 61 64
Rooms filled with Clérissy blue china as well as contemporary local ceramics.

Musée de la Poterie
Rue Sicard
06600 **Vallauris**
Tel: 04 93 64 66 51

**Musée de la Faïence
Château Pastré**
155, Avenue de Montredon
13008 **Marseilles**
Tel: 04 91 72 43 47
The museum housing this extraordinary collection of the best-known antique Marseilles faïence and Provençal ceramics (late 17th–19th centuries) is located in a lovely park between sea and hills.

**Musée des Arts et
Traditions Populaires
du Château Gombert**
5, Place des Héros
13013 **Marseilles**
Tel: 04 91 68 14 38
The very rich collections of Provençal costumes and furnishings deserve a detour.

Museon Arlaten
29, Rue de la République
13200 **Arles**
Tel: 04 90 93 58 11
Exceptional folk art and traditions, antique pottery, and Provençal costumes.

**Musée de la Poterie
Méditerranéenne,
Maison de la Terre**
Rue de la Fontaine

30700 **St-Quentin-la-Poterie**
Tel: 04 66 03 65 86

**Musée des Faïences
de Varages**
12, Place de la Libération
83670 **Varages**
Tel: 04 94 77 60 39
Three centuries of faïences
and a retrospective of
production and manu-
facturing techniques.
Photos p. 118

Musée des Faïences
Vieux Château
84240 **la Tour-d'Aigues**
Tel: 04 90 07 50 33
A collection of faïence and
porcelain produced in this village in the 18th century, as
well as pieces from Marseilles
and Moustiers.

Musée Municipal d'Apt
Rue de l'Amphithéâtre
84400 Apt
Tel: 04 90 74 78 45
Huge collection of about
400 pieces of 18th- and 19th-
century faïence.

PEWTER

Valérie Debuisson
Route de Lac
83570 **Carcès**
Tel: 04 94 04 37 33
One of the last pewterware
makers, working in a lovely
village. Made-to-order
dishes, platters, tureens,
candelabra, etc., cast from
antique molds.

GLASSWARE

La Verrerie de Biot
5, Chemin des Combes
06410 **Biot**
Tel: 04 93 65 03 00
Pale colored, handmade
glassware made by master
craftsmen.

V. TRADITIONAL FABRICS

ANTIQUE FABRICS

La Maison du Boutis
9, Place du Général-de-Gaulle
30420 **Calvisson**
Tel: 04 66 01 63 75
Local collection of 18th- and
19th-century painting.

Musée du Costume Comtadin
84210 **Pernes-les-Fontaines**
Tel: 04 90 61 31 04
Museum of traditional fabrics, underwear, and skirts.

Michel Garcia
20, Rue Jean-d'Autant
84360 **Lauris**
Tel: 04 90 08 36 15

La Maison Biehn
7, Avenue des Quatre-Otages
84800 **L'Isle-sur-la-Sorgue**
Tel: 04 90 20 89 04
Michel Biehn, author of
many books about Provence,
specializes in traditional,
regional, and antique fabrics.

MODERN FABRICS

Fragonard
20, Boulevard Fragonard
06130 **Grasse**
Tel: 04 93 36 44 65
This perfumer also offers a
range of quilting, reversible
counterpanes, etc.

Les Filles d'Hortensia
2, Rue de la Bibliothèque
13001 **Marseilles**
Tel: 04 91 48 44 64
Embroidered and initialed
linen in bright colors; cotton
fabric in traditional patterns
and Mediterranean blue.

Les Olivades
Chemin des Indienneurs
13103 **St-Étienne-du-Grès**
Many locations in Provence
and Paris. For a list of outlets

tel: 04 90 49 19 19.
This factory makes cottons
with traditionally inspired
patterns. Also produces
quilted comforters, throws,
quality Provençal decoration
for the table, kitchen, and
bedroom. The *Guide des Har-
monies* catalog is an excellent
source of inspiration.
Photos pp. 150 and 151

Souleiado
39, Rue Proudhon
13150 **Tarascon**
Tel: 04 90 91 08 80 for a list of
outlets in Provence and Paris.
Stylized 18th-century Indian
prints traditionally hand-
blocked with Provençal
patterns taken from nature.
Laurel, bees, and olives
feature on cretonne, percale,
and cotton muslin, sold by
the meter or made into table
linen, clothing, or objects,
some of them quilted.
*Photos pp. 29, 85, 91, 121, 130,
136–141, 145, 146, 148, and 150*

Valdrôme
5 *bis*, Rue Louis Barthou
26000 **Valence**
Tel: 04 75 43 35 05
Brightly colored cotton fabrics for bedroom and table.

Les Indiennes de Nîmes
Boutiques in Arles, Avignon,
Saint-Rémy. For more details,
tel: 04 66 83 48 40
Manufacturer of typical
Provençal textiles; also a
specialist in watchmen's
uniforms and Provençal
"Sunday best."

L'Estoffe
22, Cours Théodore-Bouge
83690 **Salernes**
Tel: 04 94 67 57 00
Fabrics sold by the meter,
plasticized tablecloths,
tablemats, napkins: a real
Aladdin's cave.

Chantal Geoffroy
83720 **Trans-en-Provence**
Tel: 04 94 67 78 79
Will travel to give groups
lectures on the technique of
making *boutis*.

Les Tissus Marinette
4, Rue Georges-Clemenceau
83990 **Saint-Tropez**
Tel: 04 94 73 31 57
Huge choice of fabrics sold
by the meter or made into
linens and clothing, a
favorite with the locals.

Édith Mézard
Château de l'Ange
84220 **Lumières**
Tel: 04 90 72 36 41
Embroidery workshop:
linen, hemp, and cotton bed-
linen, and tablecloth fabrics.

PARISIAN ADDRESSES

Cotolaine
131, Bd Sébastopol
75002 **Paris**
Tel: 01 42 33 90 96
Very reasonable prices for
boutis and piqué throws created in partnership with the
big department stores. Large
choice of patterns: stylized
floral motifs inspired by
18th- and 19th-century patterns, in popular modern
colorways as well as in a
range of undyed fabrics.
Outlets throughout France,
including at Rêves, Marseille
(Tel: 04 91 37 66 60), at La
Maison de Marion at Les
Baux-de-Provence (04 90 54
34 41), Le Rideau de Paris,
and branches of Printemps.

Michèle Aragon
21, Rue Jacob
75006 **Paris**
Tel: 01 43 25 87 69
Huge choice of colored,
flower-patterned *boutis*.

Blanc d'Ivoire
—104, Rue du Bac
75007 **Paris**
Tel: 01 45 44 41 17
—4, Rue Jacob
75006 **Paris**
Tel: 01 46 33 34 29
The catalog offers a handsome choice of reversible quilted coverlets.

Villaret
13, Rue Oberkampf
75011 **Paris**
Tel: 01 40 21 71 89
Quilted coverlets embroidered with friezes of greenery or little roses.

Elsa C.
171, Rue du Fbg-St-Antoine
75011 **Paris**
Tel: 01 44 75 78 85
Provençal stores give pride of place to the quilted comforters of this designer.

Mis en Demeure
27, Rue du Cherche-Midi
75006 **Paris**
Tel: 01 45 48 83 79
This designer calls his quilts *boutis*. Even though this is not the correct term, they are nonetheless attractive.

Le Rideau de Paris
32, Rue du Bac
75007 **Paris**
Tel: 01 42 61 18 56
Florence Maeght runs this company, which produces *boutis* to order. These creations are based on her collection of 18th- and 19th-century Provençal textiles. There is a handsome choice of quilted coverlets, whose exclusive designs are still hand-blocked or produced from reproductions of traditional Provençal fabrics.
Photos pp. 142, 143, 146, and 147

VI. IN THE GARDEN

FURNITURE

This section lists craftsmen who make wrought-iron garden furniture, verandas, and pergolas; they could as easily produce wrought-ironwork for interiors, stair-rails, balustrading, etc.

La Forge d'Opio
4, Chemin des Eigages
06650 **Opio**
Tel: 04 93 77 24 90
Garden furniture, lamps, candelabra decorated with foliage, curlicues, etc.

Jean-Marie Bonnefoy
Le Revest,
chemin départemental 14
Puyricard
13100 **Aix-en-Provence**
Tel: 04 42 92 10 31
Ironwork and locksmithing in the traditional way.

La Forge du Roy René
11, Square Voltaire
13150 **Tarascon**
Tel: 04 90 91 20 00
Restoration of listed buildings, such as the 18th-century staircase of the Mas des Comtes at Tarascon.

Jean-Claude Guigne
4, Place Émile-Combes
13150 **Tarascon**
Tel: 04 90 91 04 99
Provençal ladders, for picking fruits and olives, need to be very tall. This craftsman carries on the ancient tradition of making such ladders.

Unopiu'
286, Avenue du Millet
13782 **Aubagne Cedex**
Tel: 04 42 18 60 80
Wrought-iron and wooden garden furniture, garden pottery, iron pergolas, bowers—everything for decorating and shading a terrace. Full catalog available upon request.

Pépinières Jean-Marie Rey
Route de La Londe-les-Plages
83250 **La Londe-les-Maures**
Tel: 04 94 05 17 87
A huge private nursery that offers olive, cypress, and oleander trees, plus garden furniture and ornaments.

Tendance Métal
2144, Chemin Long
83260 **La Crau**
Tel: 04 94 57 85 80
Creator of antiqued wrought-iron furniture for indoors and out.

Christian Hoogewys
Zone artisanale
Route de Collobrières
83310 **Cogolin**
Wrought-ironwork.

Silvacanne
Les Cavaliers Nord
83320 **Carqueiranne**
Tel: 04 94 58 50 09
For three generations, the Donati family has been growing reeds near Hyères, in one of the best reed-beds in the world. The family provides reeds for some of the world's greatest clarinettists and saxophonists; they are also the last makers of the *canisses*, which filter sunlight to provide shade for garden terraces. Pergolas and enclosures are another speciality of this company.

Ferronnerie Cassien
Fontaine de la Daby
83330 **Le Beausset**
Tel: 04 94 98 70 73
Porticos, bowers, iron staircases, balconies, etc.

Hervé Baume
6, Rue de la Grande-Fusterie
84000 **Avignon**
Tel: 04 90 86 61 24

This elegant store sells wrought-iron garden furniture, as well as lovely indoor furniture and objects.

Claude Briquet
Avenue du 8-Mai
84150 **Jonquières**
Tel: 04 90 70 61 22
Ironwork (doors, tables, chairs, stair-rails), copies of antique items, or designs made to order.

La Forge
11, Chemin des Paluds
84210 **Valayans**
Tel: 04 90 62 03 81
Ironwork, restoration of antique items.

Gérard Aude
84220 **Saint Pantaléon**
Tel: 04 90 72 22 67
Tables, garden chairs; this ironmonger can assemble furniture that will allow you to enjoy your garden through the winter months.
Photos pp. 168 et 169

Jean Féraud
Boulevard Roumanille
84260 **Sarrians**
Tel: 04 90 65 41 37
A highly skilled ironmonger who creates garden furniture, arches, or gates.

Ferronerie Mathieu
Chemin de Saint-Roch
84360 **Lauris**
Tel: 04 90 08 25 62
Produces stairways, gates, balconies.

La Forge des Templiers
Route de Grillon
84600 **Richerenches**
Tel: 04 90 28 01 72
Wrought-ironwork.
EARTHENWARE JARS

Lei Noues Trei Viei
614, Route de la Mer
06410 **Biot**

Tel: 04 93 65 02 05
Antique store specializing in biotoises jars, kitchenware.

Les Jarres de Provence
1449, Route de la Mer
06410 **Biot**
Traditional pottery jars.

Poterie Provençale Augé-Laribé
1689, Route de la Mer
06410 **Biot**
Tel: 04 93 65 63 30
Jars, bowls, and garden urns.

Poterie de la Méditerranée
Avenue des Caniers
Tel: 04 42 82 40 00
or Avenue des Goumes
Tel: 04 42 18 79 79.
13400 **Aubagne**
Wide choice of garden pots and urns in unglazed clay.

Terres de Provence
100, Avenue de Coulin
13420 **Gémenos**
Tel: 04 42 32 04 00
Pottery and garden urns.

**Poterie d'Anduze
Les Enfants de Boisset**
30140 **Anduze**
Tel: 04 66 61 80 86
This where the *vases d'Anduze* pots are made. There are often long delays on orders.

Poterie La Madeleine
30140 **Tornac**
Tel: 04 66 61 63 44
Large-size *vases d'Anduze* made in the traditional way.

Raison de plus
371, Route d'Uzès
30700 **St-Quentin-la-Poterie**
Tel: 04 66 22 58 70
Studio potter, making vases, ceramics, and jars.

Jean-Claude Appy
Route de Joucas,
Quartier Trabail
84200 **Roussillon**

Tel: 04 90 05 62 94
A wide choice of garden pottery and furniture, as well as trees and plants.

Michel Cayla
9, Rue des Artisans
84210 **Saint-Didier**
Tel: 04 90 66 11 60
Wonderful jars, terra-cotta table-bases and statues.

CALADES

Les Tapis de Galet
29, Avenue Parc Laval
06600 **Antibes**
Tel: 06 11 16 96 65
François Dovillez creates magnificent pebble carpets to decorate terraces, but can also produce simple pathways using colored pebbles to create a geometric design.

LANDSCAPE ARTIST

Dingwall Maine
Landscape Enterprise Ltd.
84480 **Lacoste**
Tel: 04 90 75 86 34
Landscaper and creator of gardens; author of *The Luberon Garden*, published by Ebury Press, London, UK.
p. 157

VII. GUESTHOUSES AND HOTELS OF DISTINCTION

Bastides, *farmhouses*, mas, *village houses, little châteaux, windmills*, mazets, *villas, sheepfolds: these guesthouses and hotels of distinction offer the visitor the pleasure of living in a typical Provençal house.*

Rue du Château
13150 **Tarascon**
Tel: 04 90 91 09 99
Guesthouse in the old part of town, rooms surround a lovely ocher-walled patio.
Photos p. 46

Mas dou Pastre
13810 **Eygalières**
Tel: 04 90 95 92 61
Originally a shepherd's house, this is now a very comfortable hostelry.

L'Anastasy
Île de la Barthelasse
84000 **Avignon**
Tel: 04 90 85 55 94
Farmhouse popular with theater people because of the hostess, Olga Manguin.
Photos pp. 104 and 156

Hôtel de La Mirande
4, Place Amirande
84000 **Avignon**
Tel: 04 90 85 93 93
A magnificent example of authentic 18th-century architecture and interiors.

La Combe
Chemin de Sainte-Croix
84110 **Vaison-la-Romaine**
Tel: 04 90 28 73 70
A delightful building set among vineyards.

Villa Saint-Louis
35, Rue Henri-de-Savornin
84160 **Lourmarin**
Tel: 04 90 68 39 18
Handsome 17th-century house, once a family home.

La Maison aux Volets Bleus
84201 **Venasque**
Tel: 04 90 66 03 04
Rooms with a view over Mont Ventoux in a delightful village.

Le Mas des Falaises
84210 **Le Beaucet**
Tel: 04 90 74 15 71
This lovely house belongs to the Société Boiseries et Décorations. It can only be rented as a single unit (6 bedrooms).

**L'Atelier du peintre
Chez Hervé Thibault**
Hameau des Beaumettes
84220 **Gordes**
Tel: 04 90 72 27 53
The painter Hervé Thibault and his wife Marie have decorated this house in an original way that reflects their own taste and love of color.
Photos pp. 46, 67, 81, 83, and 90

La Maison
84340 **Beaumont-du-Ventoux**
Tel: 04 90 65 15 50
Small, 18th-century farmhouse, whose rooms are decorated in the Provençal style.

La Carraire
84360 **Lauris**
Tel: 04 90 08 36 89
Delightful 17th-century farmhouse with stunning views.
Photos pp. 22–23

La Maison des Sources
Chemin des Fraisses
84360 **Lauris**
Tel: 04 90 08 22 19
A stone house with a terrace shaded by an acacia tree.

Hôtellerie de Crillon le Brave
84410 **Crillon le Brave**
Tel: 04 90 65 61 61
The warmth and comfort of a Provençal country farm is offered in these village houses nestling by the church.

Le Mourre
84580 **Oppede-le-Vieux**
Tel: 04 90 76 99 31
A dovecote, an old grain mill, and guest rooms are situated among vines and fig trees near this pretty village.

INTERNATIONAL SUPPLIERS OF PROVENÇAL GOODS

Following is a list of addresses for those interested in purchasing Provençal goods outside of France. It is intended as a guide only, and is by no means exhaustive.

UNITED STATES

Another Time, Another Place, Inc.
11811 South Street
Louisville, CO 80027
Tel: (1) 720-890-7700
www.atapantiques.com
Good range of enamelware, woodenware, metalware, pottery, textiles, garden goods, etc.

Belle Provence
P.O. Box 2854
Rohnert Park, CA 94927-2854
www.belleprovence.com
Regional items from southern France including handmade Provençal tablecloths.

Bonjour Provence
www.bonjourprovence.com
Website featuring a range of Provençal goods.

D'Avignon
P.O. Box 156
Wilton, CT 06897-0156
Toll free: (1) 877-417-2158
www.davignonstore.com
Provençal goods sold on-line.

Édith Mézard
Available through:
French Look International, Inc.
233 N. California
Chicago, IL 60612
Tel: (1) 773-722-8200
Fax: (1) 773-772-8201
www.frenchlookint.com
Provençal fabrics—see French addresses for details.

Elsa C.
Available through:
Village de Provence
169 Crossroads Blvd
Carmel, LA 9323
Tel: (1) 831-626-9425
www.villageprovence.com
Provençal fabrics—see French addresses for details.

L'Estoffe
Available through:
www.arithisia.fr
Provençal fabrics—see French addresses for details.

French Country Antiques
1000 King Street
Alexandria, VA 22314
Tel: (1) 703-548-8563
Fax: (1) 703-548-8563
Bedwarmers, painted chairs, enamelware, 19th- century mirrors, etc.

French Fabrics
www.french-fabrics.com
Toile de Jouy by the yard, as well as French lace and trimmings, tableware, accessories, linens, and wallpapers.

The Gables Antiques
711 Miami Circle NE
Atlanta, GA 30324
Tel: (1) 404-231-0734
Fax: (1) 404-231-0749
www.thegablesantiques.com
Specialize in 18th- and 19th-century country French furniture. Features a wide range of Provence-style items.)

Les Indiennes de Nîmes
U.S. Agent: M. Vacherie
Tel: (1) 404-816-7825
Provençal fabrics—see French addresses for details.

Maison d'Arceaux
Toll free: (1) 877-475-0087
www.maisondar.com
Small, family-owned firm specializing in high-quality French linens.

Les Olivades
U.S. Agent: **Pierre Deux**
(see below)
www.les-olivades.com
Provençal fabrics—see French addresses for details.

Pierre Deux
www.pierredeux.com
Tel: 1-888-PIERRE-2 (743-7732)
Specializes in the design and recreation of 18th- and 19th-century French fabrics, accessories, and furnishings.

La Provence
239 Chartres Street
New Orleans, LA 70130
Tel: (1) 504-299-0772
Fax: (1) 504-299-0773
www.provencelinens.com
Provence-style tablecloths, towels, and napkins.

Rue de France
www.ruedefrance.com
A wide range of goods from Provençal linens through to children's-wear and lighting.

Soleil en Provence
402 Washington Street
Wellesley, MA 02482
Tel: (1) 781-239-1101
www.provence-shop.com
A wide range of handcrafted Provençal goods.

Souleiado
102-A Main Street
Northeast Harbor, ME 04662
Tel: (1) 207-276-3828
Toll free: 888-855-2828
Provençal fabrics—see French addresses for details.

Les Tissus de Provence
www.tissusdeprovence.com
Provençal fabric by the meter, curtains, tablecloths, etc.

Valdrôme
Available in outlets in the U.K. and U.S.
www.valdrome.com.

Provençal fabrics—see French addresses for details.

Village Français
10 Long Hill Road
Guilford, CT 06437
Tel: (1) 203-458-1800
Fax: (1) 203-458-0615
Country furniture from the 17th-, 18th-, and 19th-century.

UNITED KINGDOM

Lantiques
Lurgashall
West Sussex, England
Tel: +44 (0)1730 810 340 or +44 (0)7785 755 167
www.lantiques.com
Supplier of authentic French provincial antiques.

LP Antiques
The Old Brewery
Short Acre Street
Walsall, England
Tel:+44 (0)1922 746 764
Fax:+44 (0)1922 611 316
French antique furniture.

Les Olivades
Mail order only.
Tel: +44 (0)207 731 0444
Fax: +44 (0)207 731 0788
www.les-olivades.com

Pugh's Antiques
Tel: +44 (0)1404 42860
www.pughs-antiques-export.com
Range includes a selection of antique Provençal furniture.

CANADA

En Provence Inc.
20 Hazelton Avenue
Toronto, Ontario
Tel: (1) 416-975-9400
French country furnishings, decor, and design.

L'Esprit de Provence
www.lespritprovence.com
A huge range of Provençal goods; Provençal recipes.

BIBLIOGRAPHY

General titles:
• Chamberlain, Samuel. *Domestic Architecture in Rural France*. Architectural Book Publishing Company, 1981.
• Jones, Louisa. *Provence: A Country Almanac*. Stewart, Tabori & Chang, 1999.
• Laws, Bill. *Traditional Houses of Rural France*. Abbeville Press, 1997.
• Lovatt-Smith, Lisa ed. and Muthesius, A. ed. *Provence Interiors/Interieurs De Provence (in English)*. Taschen, 1997.
• More, Julian. *Tour de Provence*. Trafalgar Square, 2001.
• Phillips, Betty Lou and Pissack, Dan. *Provençal Interiors: French Country Style in America*. Gibbs Smith, 1998.
• Toman, Rolf. *Provence-Art: Architecture and Landscape*. Könemann, 2000.
• Williams, Roger and Brown, Deni. *Provence and Côte d'Azur*. Dorling Kindersley, 1997.

Guides to the Region:
• Coons, Nancy and Franken, Owen (photographer). *Fodor's Escape to Provence*. Fodor's Travel Publications, Fabrizio La Rocca, 2000.
• Hachette Routard: *Provence & the Côte d'Azur*. Cassell & Co, 2002.
• Michelin Green Guide: *Provence*. Michelin Travel Publications, 2000.

French-language titles:
• Beaumelle, M-J., Guerre, G. and V. and Jaquenoud, P. *Les Arts décoratifs en Provence du XVIIe au XIX siècle*. Édisud, 1993.
• Bernard, Paul. *Faïences et faïenciers de Varages*. Available at the Musée de la Faïence at Varages.
• Biehn, Michel. *Secrets d'Arlésiennes*. Actes Sud, 1999.
• Boucher, Roseline. *Les Tissus de Provence*. Éditions Aubanel, 1999.
• Bourgeois, J-J. *L'Âge d'or du siège paillé*. Éditions Massin, 1997.
• Dumas, Marc. *La Faïence d'Apt et de Castellet*. Édisud, 1992.
• Ferriol, Élisabeth. *Lumière, boutis et couverture piquée*. La Bibliothèque des métiers, 1999.
• Ferriol, Élisabeth. *Le Manuel de boutis de Madame Gaussen et 102 motifs de boutis*. La Bibliothèque des métiers, 1998.
• Mannoni, E. *Mobilier provençal*. Éditions Massin, 1995.
• Massot, J-L. *Les Maisons de Provence*. Éditions Eyrolles, 1997.
• Massot, J-L. *Maisons rurales et vie paysanne en Provence*. Éditions Berger-Levrault, 1995.
• Maurières, Arnaud and Rey, Jean-Marie. *Le Jardinier de Provence et des régions méditerranéennes*. Édisud, 1995.
• Mihière, G. *Les Bastides marseillaises*. Éditions J. Laffitte, 1993.
• Nicolle, Francine. *Boutis des ville et boutis des champs*. Édisud, 1999.
• Raulin, Henri. *Architecture rurale : Provence-Côte d'Azur : Alpes-de-Haute-Provence, Alpes-Maritimes, Bouches-du-Rhône, Var, Vaucluse*. Éditions Bonneton, 1996.
• De Rességuier, B. and Servel, B. *Les Faïences de Moustiers*. Éditions Ouest-France, 1996.
• Scheibli, Isabelle and Alain. *Faïences et poteries provençale*. A.Scheibli Éditions, 1996.
• Tripard, Vincent. *Ocres et peintures décoratives de Provence*. Édisud, 2000.

Titles from Flammarion:
• Baussan, Olivier, Meulien, Jean-Marie, and Vaillant, Jean-Charles. *Flavors of the Mediterranean*. Flammarion, 2005.
• Biehn, Michel. *Colors of Provence*. Flammarion, 2006.
• Cros, Philippe. *The Painters of Provence*. Flammarion, 2001.
• Hernandez, Florence. *Wine Tours in the South of France*. Flammarion, 2005.
• Jones, Louisa and Motte, Vincent. *Gardens in Provence*. Flammarion, 2002.
• Jones, Louisa and Motte, Vincent. *Gardens of the French Riviera*. Flammarion, 2002.
• McDowell, Dane and Sarramon, Christian. *Living in Provence*. Flammarion, 2003.
• Sibuet, Jocelyne, Deydier, Catherine, and de Laubier, Guillaume. *A French Country Home*. Flammarion, 2005.

ACKNOWLEDGEMENTS

The authors and publishers would like to thank the owners of all the houses illustrated in this book, as well as the craftspeople whose work they were allowed to photograph. They include the Marquis and Marquise de Barbentane, Pierre Bergé, Michel Biehn, Jean-François Boudin of Les Olivades, Comte and Comtesse de La Bouillerie, Jean-Jacques Bourgeois, Jean-Claude Brialy, Peggy Brozek, Madame Chancel at Val Joanis, Michel Cuxac at La Carraire, Anne Dargent, Pierre Degrugillier, Mireille Desana, Madame de Welle of the Hôtel d'Olivary, Jean Faucon, Élizabeth Ferriol of the Musée Souleiado, Martine de Fontanes, Olga Forest, Francis Guaré, Alain Gauthey, Édith Haegel, Étienne Jamet, Alain Laurens, Florence Maeght, Dingwall Maine, Olga Manguin, Édith Mézard, Jacqueline Morabito, Comte and Comtesse Morand, Monsieur Offner, Jean-Marie Rey, Comte and Comtesse de Sabran Pontevès, Anne Saurin, Hervé Thibault, Christian Tortu, Monsieur and Madame Van Tigghem, and Madame Zic of the Château de Lourmarin.

They would also like to thank Albine Harent, Nicolas Lefort, and Tatiana Nadin for assisting with the production of this book. Christian Sarramon would especially like to thank Daouia Bellal and Didier Tisseyre, Pierre Bel, Ysabel de Roquette, and Inès.

Art director: Karen Bowen

Translated from the French by Josephine Bacon, American Pie, London

Edited by Penelope Isaac

Originally published as *La Maison Provençale*

© Flammarion S.A. 2001

English-language edition

© Flammarion 2002

ISBN: 978-2-0801-0839-5

FA0839-02-II

Dépôt légal: 4/2002

Color separation: Sele Offset

07 08 09 6 5 4

Printed in Singapore by Tien Wah Press